Screenplay Library
Edited by Matthew J. Bruccoli

Previous Titles

The Asphalt Jungle. Ben Maddow and John Huston

The Blue Dahlia. Raymond Chandler

F. Scott Fitzgerald's Screenplay for "Three Comrades."
By Erich Maria Remarque

The Naked City. Albert Maltz and Malvin Wald

On the Waterfront. Budd Schulberg

San Francisco. Anita Loos

THE ROAD TO GLORY

A Screenplay

By Joel Sayre
and William Faulkner

Afterword by George Garrett

Southern Illinois University Press
Carbondale and Edwardsville

Edited by Stephen W. Smith
Designed by Gary Gore

Library of Congress Cataloging in Publication Data

Sayre, Joel, 1900–
  The road to glory.

  (Screenplay library)
  I. Faulkner, William, 1897–1962, joint author.
II. Road to glory. [Motion picture] III. Title.
IV. Series.
PN1997.R57523   791.43′72   80–29341
ISBN 0–8093–0995–5
ISBN 0–8093–0996–3 (pbk.)

Contents

Acknowledgments

The editor is indebted to Patricia A. Bower of Twentieth Century-Fox for crucial assistance. Mrs. Ben Hamilton (Hampton Books) provided the illustrations.

Faulkner at Warner Bros. in 1944, by Stephen Longstreet. *Bruccoli Collection*

The Road to Glory

[Wooden Crosses]

A Screenplay by

Joel Sayre &

William Faulkner

Credits

The Road to Glory, from a story and screenplay by Joel Sayre and William Faulkner; directed by Howard Hawks; produced by Darryl F. Zanuck for Twentieth Century-Fox.

Lieutenant Michel Denet [Pierre Delaage]	Frederic March
Captain Paul La Roche [Paul Morache]	Warner Baxter
Papa La Roche [Old Man]	Lionel Barrymore
Monique	June Lang
Bouffiou	Gregory Ratoff
Regnier	Victor Killan
Relief Captain	Paul Stanton
Duflous	John Qualen
Lieutenant Tannen	Julius Tannen
Major	Theodore Von Eltz
Rigaud	Paul Fix
Ledoux	Leonid Kinskey
Courier	Jacques Vanaire
Nurse	Edythe Raynore
Old Soldier	George Warrington

Monique's surname, which is given in the screenplay as Achard and La Coste, has been regularized to Achard. The names of some minor characters were also changed between this screenplay and the final shooting script.

The Road to Glory

FADE IN:

1 MEDIUM CLOSE SHOT STATUE "FRANCE AROUSED"
(STOCK C. de B.)* DAY
On the sound track are heard the strains of "La Marseillaise"
played with military thunder. It continues at various pitches and
tempos to the Fade Out.

DISSOLVE TO:

2 FULL SHOT PARADE GROUND (STOCK C. de B.) DAY
showing ranks of recruits presenting arms.

DISSOLVE TO:

3 MEDIUM SHOT TROOP TRAIN (STOCK C. de B.) DAY
showing the flower-bedecked soldiers leaning out of the cattle cars
and waving at the cheering crowd which throngs the platform.

DISSOLVE TO:

4 MEDIUM SHOT LOW SETUP ARTERIAL ROAD (STOCK C.
de B.) DAY
showing heavy artillery moving up.

5 MEDIUM LONG SHOT ARTERIAL ROAD (STOCK C. de B.)
DAY
showing a column of same going up the road.

DISSOLVE TO:

6 MEDIUM SHOT STREET CORNER OF BASE TOWN (STOCK
C. de B.) DAY

*Twentieth Century-Fox acquired *Les Croix de Bois*, a 1932 French movie directed by
Raymond Bernard, for its battle footage.

showing a train of horse-drawn vehicles very like covered wagons, filled with soldiers.

FADE OUT:

FADE IN:

7 INT FARM COURTYARD DAY
This is a billet. CAMERA PANS AROUND showing soldiers sitting about shaving, hunting bugs, oiling their rifles, shining their boots, etc. They are obviously veterans, and tough-looking ones at that. Bouffiou, the captain's orderly and an amiable ruffian, turns the crank of the farm pump as he leads the singing.

(NOTE: This song runs all through *Les Croix de Bois*, was doubtless a favorite in the French Army and probably has no more copyright than "Good Morning, Mr. Zip-Zip-Zip.")

BOUFFIOU

   (singing)
Going up to Montmartre
Montmartre in Paree
I came across a pretty gal
And took her on my knee.

SOLDIERS

   (singing)
Good times are here, ta-da-da-da,
Good times are here, there's wine and beer
And good times for all the gals.

BOUFFIOU

   (singing)
I asked the sergeant major,
"Can I have a pass?"
"No, you dirty soldier,
You can—"
He sees something off and stops.

BOUFFIOU

   (continuing)
'Ten-shun!
He salutes. The other men spring to attention.

8 MEDIUM LONG SHOT   GATE OF FARM COURTYARD
SOLDIERS' ANGLE
A hearse is driving slowly by. It stops. Inside the hearse is a great
mound of flowers.

9 MEDIUM CLOSE SHOT   HEARSE COACHMAN
a boozy-looking old man with a patent leather hat and enormous
moustachios.

> COACHMAN
>> (raucously)
> Hey, is this the Second Battalion of the Thirty-ninth?

> SOLDIER'S VOICE OFF
>> (awed)
> Yes, sir.

> COACHMAN
> The Fifth Company?

10 MEDIUM SHOT   GROUP SOLDIERS
staring off at the hearse and then at each other in wild surmise.

> BOUFFIOU
>> (swallowing)
> Yes, this is the Fifth.

11 THE HEARSE

> COACHMAN
> Good!

He spits, clucks at the horses and gives them a touch of the whip.
CAMERA TRUCKS AND PANS with the hearse as it rolls into the
courtyard and stops at a horse trough. The soldiers gather slowly
about it. The coachman wraps his reins around the whipstock and
climbs down from his seat. He loosens the checkreins of the
horses, which instantly plunge their noses into the trough. The
horses are in a lather. The coachman wipes his brow. He speaks in
the matter-of-fact tone of a brewery wagon driver.

> COACHMAN
> Pheew! Thirty kilos since dawn,
> gallopin' all the way.

The soldiers react.

>   BOUFFIOU
>   (gesturing at hearse)
>   But . . . but the funeral . . .
>   the body!

>   COACHMAN
>   Oh, yes—

CAMERA PANS with him as he goes to the side of the hearse and raps on the glass with his knuckles.

12 MEDIUM CLOSE SHOT INT HEARSE
with the faces of the coachman, Bouffiou, and the soldiers in the F.G. The flowers begin to twitch as the coachman continues to knock, and out of their midst rises the head of Lieutenant Pierre Delaage. He is wearing an officer's cap. He blinks, looks about him, and moves his lips in a way to indicate a dark brown taste. He looks at the flowers which cover him and reacts, then turns his head and looks through the glass, taking it big.

13 MEDIUM SHOT GROUP SOLDIERS AND COACHMAN
DELAAGE'S ANGLE
The coachman beams and raises his hat. The soldiers' eyes bug out. The coachman is seen moving toward the rear door of the hearse.

14 CLOSE SHOT DELAAGE SOLDIERS' ANGLE
He throws back his head and roars with laughter at the soldiers. His laughter is deadened by the hearse glass.

15 GROUP SHOT SOLDIERS DELAAGE'S ANGLE
They throw back their heads and roar. Their laughter is also deadened.

16 MEDIUM CLOSE SHOT INT HEARSE
SHOOTING at rear doors. The coachman swings them open and bows.

COACHMAN

End of the line, Lieutenant.

Delaage turns and looks at him. His speech is just the least bit thick.

DELAAGE

(politely)
Pardon me—but do I happen to be dead?

COACHMAN

(chuckling)
Oh, no, sir. You was just took a little dizzy.

DELAAGE

Thank you.

He reaches his right hand out to the coachman, who clasps it and pulls him from among the flowers.

17   MEDIUM SHOT   REAR OF HEARSE

The coachman helps Delaage out. Delaage brushes flowers off his uniform and shakes a garland out of the inside of his cap.

DELAAGE

(to coachman)
Thought I'd died and come back a fish in the aquarium.

COACHMAN

(laughing)
No, sir, just the Fifth Company, Second Battalion, Thirty-ninth Regiment.

Delaage pulls out a wallet.

DELAAGE

You're the greatest corpse hauler in France.

COACHMAN

(pleased)
Thank you, sir.

DELAAGE

How much?

> COACHMAN
>
> Nothing, sir. Your old regiment paid the fare. I've got your kit and overcoat on the seat.

18 MEDIUM SHOT GROUP SOLDIERS
looking at each other and trying to keep from exploding. Bouffiou steps forward.

> BOUFFIOU
>
> 'Ten-shun!

The men spring to.

19 MEDIUM CLOSE SHOT DELAAGE
The coachman is bowing out of the shot with a tip in his hand. Bouffiou comes in and salutes.

> BOUFFIOU
>
> Morning, sir. I'm Captain Morache's runner.

Delaage returns the salute.

> DELAAGE
>
> Oh, good morning.
> (to men)
> Carry on, men. . . .
> (to Bouffiou)
> Is the captain in?

> BOUFFIOU
>
> Yes, sir, but he's busy.

> DELAAGE
>
> Tell him Lieutenant Delaage, his new platoon commander, awaits his convenience.

> BOUFFIOU
>
> Yes, sir.

He salutes and runs out of shot.

20 MEDIUM SHOT GROUP SOLDIERS
They have resumed their shaving, bug hunting, rifle cleaning, etc. Delaage strolls in. The men start to come to attention.

> DELAAGE

As you were. As you were.

The men carry on.

> DELAAGE
> (continuing)

Anybody here got a drink? My tongue's like a piece of tile.

The men look at each other. One reaches down beneath a rustic table and brings up three or four canteens. He puts each to his ear and shakes it until he finds one which evidently contains some liquid. This he hands to Delaage.

> DELAAGE

Wait a minute—is this the last?

> SOLDIERS
> (ad lib.)

That's all right, sir. . . .
Go ahead. . . .
Bung 'er down, sir.

> DELAAGE

Thanks. I'll save *your* lives some day.

As he is about to drink, the hearse rolls up and the coachman doffs his hat.

> COACHMAN

Bye, sir. A pleasure to of drove you.

> DELAAGE
> (bowing)

My pleasure. We'll repeat it when I really *am* dead.

The hearse rolls off. Delaage drinks.

21 MEDIUM SHOT ORDERLY ROOM
This is Captain Paul Morache's combination sitting room and office in the farmhouse. Behind a table which he uses for a desk, Morache is sitting, his arms about the waist of Monique Achard, who is standing beside his chair. She is holding his head against her and stroking his hair. She is wearing street dress.

22 TWO-SHOT

CAMERA TRUCKS UP

>   MORACHE
>   (sighing)
>   Oh, my dear, my dear. I do love you so, so much.

Monique fondles him and kisses him lightly on the brow.

>   MONIQUE
>   My poor, tired darling.

>   MORACHE
>   It's so wonderful to hold you like this. . . .
>   (looking up at her hungrily)
>   You do love me a little?

For an instant her face looks as though she were wondering. Then she looks down at him tenderly.

>   MONIQUE
>   Of course I do. You know I do.

>   MORACHE
>   (fiercely)
>   I love you so much I think it'll kill me.

Monique gives a little laugh and takes his face in her hands.

>   MONIQUE
>   (shaking her head at him)
>   I'm very flattered, my dear, but you have enough to
>   worry about already.

She bends down and kisses him. A loud knocking is heard on the sound track. Monique raises her eyes and then her lips. She gives a little frown of mock vexation.

>   MONIQUE
>   There's that terrible war again!

Morache scowls off at the knocking and releases her reluctantly. She steps away from him and starts tidying her hair

>   MORACHE
>   (to knocker)
>   Yes?

23 MEDIUM CLOSE SHOT EXT ORDERLY ROOM BOUFFIOU

> BOUFFIOU
>
> Bouffiou, sir. Lieutenant Delaage,
> the new officer, is here.

> MORACHE'S VOICE
>
> Tell him in a minute.

Bouffiou squats and squints through the keyhole.

> BOUFFIOU
>
> In a minute, sir?

> MORACHE'S VOICE
>
> (bellowing)
> In a minute, you idiot!

Bouffiou nods sagely.

> BOUFFIOU
>
> Right, sir. In a minute.

He rises to attention, salutes, and executes a smart right face.

24 TWO-SHOT INT ORDERLY ROOM

Morache rises. Monique looks at her wrist watch.

> MONIQUE
>
> Oh, it's late! I must be getting back.

She takes her hat from the table and puts it on. Morache puts his arm around her. CAMERA TRUCKS BACK IN FRONT of them as they walk to the door. He puts both his arms around her and looks into her eyes.

> MORACHE
>
> We're moving up at nine tonight.

> MONIQUE
>
> (softly)
> I know.

> MORACHE
>
> You do? How?

MONIQUE
From your eyes. I can always tell.
Morache shakes his head gently in wonder.

MORACHE
Well, it's not going to bother us, is it?
She lowers her eyes.

MONIQUE
No.
He forces a laugh and raises her face with a finger under her chin.
She keeps her lids lowered.

MORACHE
Just a short business trip, isn't it?
Monique gets herself under control. She raises her lids. She gives
a little smile.

MONIQUE
Just a short business trip.
Morache hugs her to him, pats her collar bone and chuckles genu-
inely this time.

MORACHE
That's my big girl.
Then he holds her away from him gently, trying to make his voice
matter-of-fact. Monique's head is lowered.

MORACHE
I'll come at six-thirty and we'll have supper, darling.
They look at each other a moment and then embrace. Her face is
in the CAMERA. It wears a look of concern.

QUICK DISSOLVE TO:

25　INT　COURTYARD　CLOSE SHOT DELAAGE
sitting on his back with his chin in his hands, staring straight before him. A low muttering is heard on the sound track. Slowly and
carefully raising his head lest it drop off, he looks in its direction.

26　MEDIUM CLOSE TRUCK SHOT　BOUFFIOU　DELAAGE'S
ANGLE
He is counting on his fingers with great deliberation as he walks
slowly along.

BOUFFIOU

Fifty-seven chimpanzees . . . fifty-eight chimpanzees
. . . fifty-nine chimpanzees. . .

WIDEN ANGLE to include Delaage sitting there watching him.
Bouffiou's voice suddenly rings out. He does not see Delaage.

BOUFFIOU

Sixty chimpanzees . . . one minute!

DELAAGE

Hide and go seek?
Bouffiou looks up just as he is about to stumble over him and puts
on the brakes.

BOUFFIOU

(saluting)
Excuse me, sir. The Captain's ready.
QUICK DISSOLVE TO:

27 THREE-SHOT INT COURTYARD
Privates Brouc, Vairon, and Lemoine are stalking vermin. Brouc,
stripped to the waist, is working on his own torso. Vairon and
Lemoine are reading their shirts.

BROUC

What do you think of our new tango dancer?

LEMOINE

Looks like hot stuff.
(chuckling)
That hearse!

VAIRON

Hope he brings one in the line.
Then we won't have to bury him.

LEMOINE

Anyway, he put up for some booze.

BROUC

That reminds me. Where's those tramps with the canteens? Drinkin' it all themselves?

> VAIRON
>
> They'll be along. . . .
>> (wistfully)
>
> Wisht I was an officer. I wouldn't have to do this.

> BROUC
>> (argumentative)
>
> Officers has bugs, same as you and me.

> LEMOINE
>
> Some don't. They don't get close enough to where there is bugs.

> BROUC
>
> Ours do.

> LEMOINE
>
> But they got somebody to hunt 'em for 'em.

> VAIRON
>> (to Brouc)
>
> Besides, officers' bugs ain't as hard to catch as these.

QUICK DISSOLVE TO:

28 MEDIUM CLOSE TRUCKING SHOT MONIQUE EXT FARMHOUSE

She is hurrying along with her eyes down, fishing a handkerchief out of her pocketbook.

> DELAAGE'S VOICE
>> (softly)
>
> Drop that.

She looks up in alarm and stops.

29 CLOSE SHOT DELAAGE

grinning down at her. He has his overcoat on.

30 DELAAGE AND MONIQUE

She tries to pass but he blocks her way. He looks around to see if they are alone.

> DELAAGE
>> (rapidly)
>
> The dropping of a lady's handkerchief is the classic way to start a conversation.

MONIQUE
(trying to pass)
I don't want a conversation.
He continues to block the way.

DELAAGE
It will relax you. Have you the pen of my aunt?

MONIQUE
No, I haven't. Please let me by.

DELAAGE
(blocking her way again)
Then where can I find Captain Morache's orderly room?
She stops and glares at him.

MONIQUE
I don't know.
She tries to get by and is blocked.

DELAAGE
Well, how about your orderly room?
Monique stamps her foot in rage.

DELAAGE
(continuing)
I'd be most orderly.

MONIQUE
(furiously)
Let me pass or I shall complain to the Military Police.
Delaage steps out of her way, doffs his cap in an elaborate gesture
and bends nearly double in a bow. She sweeps by with her nose in
the air.

DELAAGE
Au revoir, mademoiselle.
He straightens up, claps his cap over his ear, grins after her and
winks.

QUICK DISSOLVE TO:

31 INT MORACHE'S ORDERLY ROOM
Morache is sitting at his desk fiddling with some papers. There is
a knock.

MORACHE

    Come in.

Delaage enters, walks up to Morache's desk and salutes. Morache rises, stretches his hand across the desk, shakes hands perfunctorily, and sits down. Delaage stands at attention.

MORACHE

(very brisk)

    Lieutenant Delaage? You're half a day late. Something wrong with the transportation?

Delaage is dabbing at his forehead with his handkerchief.

DELAAGE

Well, sir, it wasn't *quite* up to snuff.

MORACHE

Hmm. Too bad. All our replacements are late. Roads are getting so clogged these days the traffic moves along like a hearse.

DELAAGE

. . . Yes, sir.

MORACHE

Well, I'm glad you're here. We're moving up at nine tonight. I had intended to give you Number Four Platoon, but I think I'll shift Charpentier to Number Four and give you his—Number Two.

(picking up some papers)

Your old colonel's letter says in civil life you were a pianist?

DELAAGE

(wiping brow)

Yes, sir.

Morache's lip curls slightly. He looks back at the letter, then throws it down.

MORACHE

He writes nice things about you but—well, frankly, I don't think Number Four Platoon should be commanded by a pianist.

CAMERA HOLDS on Morache during the rest of this speech.

MORACHE
(continuing)
This is a tough regiment you have come to, Lieutenant, and I'm proud to say my company's the toughest in the battalion. If there's a particularly nasty piece of salient Brigade Headquarters wants held or straightened out, they send for us.

He shoots a look at Delaage.

32 CLOSEUP DELAAGE
beginning really to sweat.

33 CLOSE SHOT MORACHE
He looks Delaage up and down, then goes on.

MORACHE
Number Four Platoon specializes in trench-raiding. Its last commander was killed on a German fire step. The men are hand-picked from the wildest, craziest ruffians in the division. Maybe they wouldn't pass at a countess's afternoon musicale, but most of them wear medals for gallantry under fire.

34 CLOSEUP DELAAGE
sweating profusely and mopping.

35 CLOSE SHOT MORACHE

MORACHE
(continuing)
However, that needn't concern you yet. All I hope is that you'll absorb the morale of the company and be a credit to us.

He looks questioningly at Delaage.

36 TWO-SHOT

DELAAGE
(faintly)
Pardon, sir, but have you a basin?

> MORACHE
> (rising, angrily)
> A basin!

> DELAAGE
> (unbuttoning overcoat)
> And a pitcher.

Morache gestures in exasperation at an old-fashioned pitcher and bowl on a wash stand against the wall by the bed. Delaage totters toward it, removing his cap, overcoat, Sam Browne and tunic in almost one motion and throwing them over a chair. He seizes the pitcher, starts to pour water in the bowl, then bends his head and lets the stream fall on it.

37 CLOSE SHOT DELAAGE AT WASH STAND
He lets the water cascade over his head until the bowl is full, puts down the pitcher, then bails water on his face with both hands. He plunges his face under water, blowing bubbles. Then he raises it and runs an octave as though he were in a shower.

> DELAAGE
> (singing)
> La, da, da, dee, da, da, da. Good!

38 CLOSE SHOT MORACHE
Reacting.

39 TWO-SHOT
Delaage straightens up, inhales and exhales deeply, then grabs a towel, dries his face. He goes to the chair and searches in his tunic pocket for a comb.

> DELAAGE
> Sorry, sir, I'm all right now. Last night the mess gave me a farewell party.

He fishes something out of his pocket, looks at it and chuckles.

> DELAAGE
> (continuing)
> They also gave me this pencil.

He hands it to Morache.

40 CLOSEUP PENCIL TOP
The metal pencil is surmounted by a little crowing rooster. Morache touches it with his forefinger.

> MORACHE'S VOICE
> Is this a symbol of *your* character?

41 TWO-SHOT
Delaage, who is combing his hair, places his other hand on his chest.

> DELAAGE
> Sir, in me you behold Delaage, the fighting piano player.

> MORACHE
> (amused)
> Indeed!

> DELAAGE
> All my life I have loved German music—except that of Richard Wagner. Bach, Beethoven, and Brahms, yes. But Wagner—definitely no.

> MORACHE
> Really!

> DELAAGE
> When an enemy shell bursts it reminds me of Wagner's trombones.
> (hands over ears)
> I fly into a frenzy. I want to shoot, stab, bomb and strangle.

> MORACHE
> (laughing)
> No!

> DELAAGE
> The Germans being a notorious race of Wagner lovers, I look on them not only as enemies of France, but as personal enemies of my own.

Morache roars with laughter and claps him on the shoulder.

> MORACHE
> My boy, I think you've come to the right place.

On the SOUND TRACK is heard the sound of a tinny pounding. Both men react.

> DELAAGE
>
> Wagner!

CAMERA PANS with them as they stride to the window.

42 MEDIUM LONG SHOT INT COURTYARD THEIR ANGLE showing a group of soldiers drinking and raising hell. The noise of the tinny pounding continues.

43 GROUP SHOT INT COURTYARD (STOCK C. de B.) DAY One soldier beats a flattened-out bully beef tin with a stick while two others do the can-can. Others cheer and drink.

(NOTE: If this shot does not match it can be copied.)

44 TWO-SHOT INT ORDERLY ROOM

> MORACHE
>
> (angry)
>
> Blast those Fourth Platoon monkeys. They're going in to-night and they're drunk already.

> DELAAGE
>
> It's my fault, sir. They bought me a drink and I bought them one back. Let me handle this as my first job.

He throws open the window and leans out.

> DELAAGE
>
> (shouting)
>
> Less noise, down there! Less noise!

The noise stops at once.

45 REVERSE ANGLE Delaage hangs out of the window. In the F.G. scattered men are seen standing at attention, facing him.

> DELAAGE
>
> (continuing)
>
> The captain and I are trying to think. And hang on to that cognac. If it snows tonight, you'll need some to rub on your feet. The stuff's worth its weight in dead Boches.

Any man who gets drunk will be shot out of the biggest
cannon we can find. Now carry on, but quietly.

He shuts the window. There is a roar of pleased laughter from the
men.

46 MEDIUM SHOT INT ORDERLY ROOM

Delaage is putting on his tunic and Sam Browne. Morache watches
him as though he liked the cut of his jib.

> DELAAGE
>
> About Number Four Platoon, sir—I wish you wouldn't
> hold the piano against me.

> MORACHE
>
> (grinning)
> All right, Delaage. Number Four it is. You take 'em in
> tonight.

> DELAAGE
>
> (adjusting cap)
> Thank you, sir. I'll see they sing Wagner when we go
> over the top.

There is a knock at the door.

> MORACHE
>
> Yes?

Bouffiou comes through the door and salutes.

> BOUFFIOU
>
> The replacements have arrived, sir.

> MORACHE
>
> Good. Tell Sergeant Breval to fall them in on the north
> side of the courtyard at once.

> BOUFFIOU
>
> (saluting)
> Yes, sir.

QUICK DISSOLVE TO:

47 INT COURTYARD DAY

CAMERA PANS with Morache and Delaage as they slowly walk
down a rank of replacements, nearly all of whom are fresh-faced

youths. Morache's manner is impersonally stern. They stop before
an old soldier.

> MORACHE
>
> How old are you, papa?

> OLD SOLDIER
>
> (hesitating)
> Forty-four, sir.

> MORACHE
>
> No! What's your real age?
> Never mind your regimental age.

> OLD SOLDIER
>
> (pleading)
> Truly, sir, I'm hardly a day over forty-four.

Morache shrugs and looks at Delaage.

> DELAAGE
>
> He must be an actor.

QUICK DISSOLVE TO:

48 MORACHE AND DELAAGE
talking together. In B.G. the replacements are drawn up.

> MORACHE
>
> I don't like these old men in the company.

> DELAAGE
>
> I think it's fine of the old boy to have joined up. He only
> wants to do his bit.

> MORACHE
>
> Of course. But old men cave in at the front. They are apt
> to lose their heads and cause casualties. I'll send him
> back tonight.

> DELAAGE
>
> Oh, let him stay. We'll find him a job peeling potatoes.

> MORACHE
>
> (coldly)
> I don't need a replacement lieutenant to tell me how to
> run my company.

Delaage looks at him a moment, then falls back a pace and salutes.

> DELAAGE
>
> Sorry, sir.

Morache returns the salute, then turns to the replacements.

> VOICE OF SERGEANT BREVAL
>
> Parade-shun!

> MORACHE
>
> Soldiers of France! You are now members of the Fifth Company of the Second Battalion of the Thirty-ninth Regiment of the Line. This regiment was created by General Bonaparte and served with him gloriously through many campaigns. It also served in the Crimea, in Indo-China, and in Africa. Since November 1914 it has been fighting on this front. Its record of valor has not yet been damaged. I do not expect any man or any platoon or even this entire company to add stature to this record, but I do and will require that no man in it will detract from it.

49 CLOSEUP DELAAGE
as he looks at Morache with genuine admiration.

50 MEDIUM CLOSE SHOT MORACHE

> MORACHE
>
> You will be assigned to platoons at once and at eight-thirty you will stand to with them in heavy packs. That is all.

A whistle trills.

> FADE OUT:

51 NIGHT
This is a scene coming up to the front. It is a background of gunfire. An almost steady sound some distance away. A hillcrest bare and jagged, silhouetted against a steady flickering of light. Against this in silhouette, the heads and shoulders of troops, helmets and rifles, etc. These men are struggling somewhat. This is Delaage's platoon. Word comes back from ahead.

> NCO WORD
>
> Close up, men—close up!

Nobody pays any attention to him. Frequently Laboussere begins to whistle the "Marseillaise" very off-key, in a plaintive tone as if he were alone. At once two savage voices speak.

VOICES

Shut up!

We pick up Laboussere. He stops whistling, on his face an expression of surprise and recollection.

LABOUSSERE

I forgot!

SECOND VOICE

If you have got to whistle, whistle the other one.

Laboussere begins to whistle "The Prisoner of Challon," still off-key in the same plaintive tone. As they advance, out of the background of shellfire comes the sound of nearer shells, from a point directly ahead. The company is approaching the registered area. The men close up. In the background the entrance to the communication trench. Shells are bursting about the entrance to the trench at 30-second intervals. This interval will be made definite. A guide in the foreground crouching and waiting. The platoon comes up. The runner challenges. Sergeant Regnier halts the platoon.

GUIDE

Fourth Platoon?

REGNIER

Yes.

GUIDE

Where's the officer?

As Sergeant Regnier turns to pass the word back, Delaage enters. The shells are still bursting. We see the men waiting, watching the shells burst. Their faces are quite grave, but quiet. The guide salutes Delaage.

GUIDE

Orders to send the platoon across in sections, Lieutenant.

DELAAGE

Yes, I know.

Delaage watches the shell burst also. His face is quite grave, too.

DELAAGE
What's the interval?

GUIDE
Thirty seconds, sir.

Delaage checks the next burst on his watch. He divides the platoon into four sections. He gets the first section ready.

DELAAGE
When I give the word, run for it.

The burst comes. He sends the first section across. The second burst comes. He sends the second section across. The next burst comes. The third section runs forward. Before they reach the communication trench, another coming out of time makes a direct hit. We will see Delaage's face as he hears the whining of the approaching shells and knows what is going to happen. We will see the faces of the men of the doomed section as they hear the shells coming and fling themselves to earth in vain. The entire section is wiped out. We see the faces of the fourth section watching—various expressions of fear and anxiety.

DELAAGE
Fourth section, forward!

He sends this section running across, himself coming last. The burst comes behind them. They are now in a communication trench.

DELAAGE
Get on—get on. You're out of danger now!

Word goes forward. The NCOs shouting and saying—

NCO
Forward, men—close up there.

Presently we hear Laboussere begin to whistle the "Marseillaise" again. At once two or three savage voices shout at him.

VOICES
Shut up! Shut up!

LABOUSSERE
Excuse me. I'll whistle the other one.

He whistles "The Prisoner of Challon." The whistling dies away.

NCO VOICES
Close up, men! Close up!

DISSOLVE TO:

52 THE FRONT LINE TRENCH NIGHT
Sentries on the fire step. The flash of shell-burst beyond the parapet. The men of the relief company are preparing to go out. One by one the sentries are relieved and step down. As the new sentries take their place.
NCOs are shouting orders. It is a scene of a sort of orderly pandemonium. As the outgoing and incoming men pass each other. All this time we have been hearing the voice of a wounded man, from beyond the parapet. The men begin to hear the voice.

LEDOUX
What is that?
We see this soldier; a nervous overstrained man—not a coward but just unfit for warfare.

REGNIER
What do you think it is? A canary? Get on into the dugout for roll call.
The men go on.

CUT TO:

53 ANOTHER PART OF TRENCH
The voice of the wounded man can still be heard. It is louder and nearer now. The captain's name is Morache. He is talking to the captain of the relieved company. They both are listening to the voice.

MORACHE
Since last night? Couldn't you get him in?
The relieved captain shrugs his shoulders. He leads Morache to a loophole in the sand bag.

RELIEVED CAPTAIN
Look!
Morache looks out and sees the wounded man caught in the wire, writhing and crying. Between the wire and the parapet are three bodies of dead soldiers. Even as Morache looks at them a burst of

machine gun bullets comes across the ground and strikes them again.

> RELIEVED CAPTAIN'S VOICE
>
> You see. We tried to get him in this morning. That's what happened to the men who went out for him.

> MORACHE
>
> Too bad they don't raise that gun a little and put him out of his misery.

> RELIEVED CAPTAIN
>
> Yes. Anyway, I'm out of mine. I won't have to listen to him any longer. Good luck.

The relieved captain goes on. The trench is relieved. The man on the wire still cries. Morache still watches him from the loophole. Sergeant Regnier, Ledoux, and others come up behind the captain. Ledoux is already talking.

> LEDOUX
>
> How do they expect us to sleep with him?—

> REGNIER
>
> You never came here to sleep. You came here to—

Regnier sees Morache.

> REGNIER
>
> (to Ledoux)
> Get on now—beat it.

Morache turns to Regnier.

> MORACHE
>
> Well, Regnier.

> REGNIER
>
> One section, sir—at the Corner.

> MORACHE
>
> Ah! Ask Lieutenant Delaage to report to me as soon as he calls his roll.

> REGNIER
>
> Very good, sir.

Regnier goes on.

CUT TO:

54 FOURTH PLATOON'S DUGOUT

The men are stowing away their gear, making themselves at home. The voice of the wounded man is very faint now, but still audible. The nervous man, Ledoux, is already talking.

LEDOUX

They don't care. They will let him hang there and suffer and suffer. Tomorrow it may be any of us. It may be me—me—me!

Regnier shuts him off. Ledoux is almost hysterical. An orderly comes down the steps.

ORDERLY'S VOICE

'Shun—officers!

The men come to attention. Delaage enters.

DELAAGE'S VOICE

At ease, men.
(to Regnier)
You have the names of Number Three Section?

REGNIER

Yes, sir.

DELAAGE

Everyone else accounted for?

REGNIER

Yes, sir.

DELAAGE

Good. You will report to the adjutant in the morning.

Regnier turns to go out. Ledoux had been watching him. Crouching. He starts forward.

LEDOUX

What about us that ain't dead yet, that have got to try to sleep here and listen to him?

Delaage turns and looks at Ledoux.

REGNIER'S VOICE

Shut up, you.

Delaage looks from face to face of the men watching him. Then he looks at Regnier, who is watching him intently.

REGNIER'S VOICE
Two men might bring him in if the Lieutenant—

DELAAGE
Might?

The sergeant does not answer. He and Delaage stare at one another.

DELAAGE
You and who else?

Ledoux springs forward.

LEDOUX
Me—me—I would rather be dead than have to—

DELAAGE
As you were.

Delaage looks out at the men who are watching him.

DELAAGE
Second section relieves at two o'clock. Stand to at four. Better get some sleep now. Come with me, Sergeant.

Delaage and Regnier go out. The men stare after them. The nervous man begins to shout and call to them.

CUT TO:

55 THE TRENCH   NIGHT
Morache is making his rounds. The wounded man's voice is louder now. Enter Delaage and Regnier.

MORACHE
Regnier says you lost a—

He looks at their faces.

MORACHE
What?

DELAAGE
That man out there. Regnier says—

MORACHE
Don't you know the other company lost three other men trying to get him this morning? I'm not going to send any of my men out there.

DELAAGE

These are volunteers.

Morache looks at Delaage and Regnier.

MORACHE

(to Regnier)

Men complaining?

Regnier shrugs.

MORACHE

Who is the other one?

DELAAGE

Why not me? We might do it, and if not, might as well
get it that way as to wait. Of course, I don't know about
Regnier, but you can get plenty more officers. Paris was
full of them last night.

Morache pays no attention to Delaage. He watches Regnier.

MORACHE

Who else, Regnier?

REGNIER

Ledoux, sir.

MORACHE

Ah—Ledoux. Well, we can spare Ledoux. But not you.
You can't go. But if you can find another volunteer to go
with Ledoux, you can try it. But just once. Tell the men
that.

REGNIER

Very good, sir.

Regnier goes out. Delaage watches Morache curiously.

DELAAGE

So we can spare Ledoux?

MORACHE

(inattentively)

If it could be done, do you think I would have waited for
volunteers? Have you looked out there?

He pauses and looks at Delaage. He has just noticed an overtone in Delaage's voice.

> MORACHE
>
> I don't think I should have needed to wait for a replacement subaltern to advise me about it anyway.

Morache and Delaage look at one another. Morache's face is cold and a little grim. Delaage's expression is flippant.

> MORACHE
>
> What was your company before this?

> DELAAGE
>
> 112th, sir.

> MORACHE
>
> Ah—evidently you are finding this one a little different?

Delaage makes a flippant gesture.

> DELAAGE
>
> Your pardon, Captain—Let it be Ledoux.
>
> DISSOLVE TO:

55A The trench directly beneath the wounded man's voice. Morache, Delaage, Regnier, and Ledoux are present. Three or four other soldiers in the background looking around and listening. Morache and Delaage are looking through the loophole. They see the man in the wire and the three dead bodies between the wire and the parapet. While they watch, the machine gun bullets rake along the ground and strike the three bodies and pass on. Behind them we hear Ledoux's voice, hysterical. Regnier is trying to make him shut up. We hear the voices of other men along the trench.

> LEDOUX
>
> I'd rather be dead than have to listen to him all night long.

> REGNIER
>
> And maybe we would rather you were dead than to have to listen all night long to you.

Ledoux is making a parcel of his belongings to leave behind him.
Regnier is standing over him.

> REGNIER
>
> Come on—come on—where do you think you are
> going?—To Berlin?

Regnier looks about at the other faces.

> REGNIER
>
> All right now—who else will volunteer?

The men hang back. At last three come forward.

> REGNIER
>
> Three is too many. The Captain says just one.

The three men look at him.

> REGNIER
>
> Then we will have to draw lots for you.

He takes a dingy, dog-eared letter from his pocket. We see the
beginning of the letter ("Dear Husband—the children are—"), and
Regnier is tearing three strips when a sentry further down the
trench speaks.

> RIGAUD
>
> Give me a relief here.

Regnier looks at him sharply.

> REGNIER
>
> Now what do you want, Rigaud? If you want to vote in
> this you can cast your vote from there.

> RIGAUD
>
> Give me a relief, I'm coming down.

Regnier turns to one of the men.

> REGNIER
>
> Relieve Rigaud, there.

Rigaud pushes into the group. He is a saturnine, grim man. He
speaks in a short, clipped voice.

> RIGAUD
>
> I'm going.

Regnier looks at him, hands on hips.

REGNIER

You are, are you? You will draw lots just like we—

RIGAUD

No—don't you remember Souchez?

Regnier pauses, looks at Rigaud a moment. His air is quiet now. He turns to Ledoux.

REGNIER

All right, Ledoux. Rigaud goes with you.

We see two other soldiers speaking aside.

FIRST SOLDIER

His brother died on the wire that way in front of Souchez, last year. Rigaud had to listen to him for two days before a barrage came.

Rigaud methodically removes his equipment. He takes from his hand a pocketful of money and gives it to Regnier.

RIGAUD

Here—but I just owe you eight francs now. If you keep out more than that—I will come back some night and frighten your cow so that she will only give buttermilk.

Regnier shoves the money back into Rigaud's pocket. His actions and voice are gruff and harsh now to hide the sentiment.

REGNIER

Do your own counting when you come back then—pig!

He is sharp, now.

REGNIER

All right—all right—men. You, Ledoux! Write your love letter tomorrow. Out with you if you are going.

Ledoux and Rigaud mount the parapet cautiously. They crouch for a moment. We can hear Ledoux's voice, still whimpering and wailing. They spring over. We see the tense faces of the men along the fence. Morache and Delaage watch through the loophole. They watch Rigaud and Ledoux crawling swiftly toward the man on the wire. We see the burst of machine gun fire come raking across the earth toward them. It catches them before they have gone ten feet. Rigaud is killed instantly. Ledoux is screaming louder than the man on the wire. The machine gun bullets travel on. Delaage whirls from the loophole. He is cursing. He climbs the parapet. Regnier grabs at his legs. Delaage kicks free. He jumps up on the parapet and drags Rigaud and Ledoux back. The men in the trench lower Ledoux to the fire step and drag Rigaud in. Delaage leaps down into the trench as the machine gun bullets rake past again. We see Morache step onto the fire step, drawing his pistol. He points it and fires swiftly three or four times. At once the voice of the man on the wire ceases. Delaage has gotten to his feet. He looks at Morache.

DELAAGE

God rest him.

Morache turns to Regnier. Ledoux is crying very loud. Regnier is kneeling beside Rigaud.

MORACHE

Send Ledoux to the rear.

Regnier rises. He shouts, harshly.

REGNIER

Well, what are you doing? What do you think this is? Do you want another man to listen to all night?

They raise Ledoux and carry him off. His crying dies away. Regnier stands looking down at Rigaud. Delaage approaches and lays his hand on Regnier's shoulder.

DELAAGE

Shall we get on with the report now?

REGNIER

Very good, sir.

Delaage and Regnier go out. The men are watching Morache. When he looks at them they turn their faces quickly away.

MORACHE

All right—men—carry on!

The men disperse. Morache stands with his head lowered, looking at the pistol. He puts it back into the holder, raises his head and moves on.

FADE OUT:

FADE IN:

56 AN EARTH WALL NIGHT

It is covered with vertical marks in rows and in sections of five. Each section has been crossed off with a lateral scratch down to the last ten sections which have not been crossed out. A hand holding a bayonet is in the act of scratching out the last section. It performs this action with a kind of ritualistic finality.

> VOICE
>
> Just fifty hours more, then we will be out again.

> SECOND VOICE
>
> —And then come back again.

> THIRD VOICE
>
> That's the reason I always hate to go out.

> SECOND VOICE
>
> Then ask the captain to let you stay—why don't you? Just stay down in this hole and grow a long white beard, and when you come out they will think you are a general and then you won't have to come back again.

> FIRST VOICE
>
> If they thought he was a general and found him up here in the front line, they would know he was crazy and then he wouldn't ever come out of any place again.

The CAMERA MOVES BACK and we see

57 THE WHOLE DUGOUT

The men preparing for bed. Some getting into the bunks. A domino game just breaking up. Now we hear the "Prisoner of Challon." We see everyone in the dugout stop everything he is doing and look toward the man who is whistling. This man holds a steel mirror before his face and by wetting his finger on his thumb, he is arranging his love-lock, turning his head this way and that. He is completely oblivious of the men who are watching him, with a sort of wolflike air and who are waiting to spring on him. He finishes "The Prisoner of Challon," then he begins to whistle the "Marseillaise," still with that pensive and depressed air as though he is not aware himself of what he is doing. At once the men start forward but Regnier stops them with a gesture. He approaches. The man still whistles. Regnier takes the man's chin in his hand and raises his face. For a moment longer, the man still whistles, even though his eyes show surprise and consternation. Then he ceases.

> LABOUSSERE'S VOICE
> I forgot. I thought I was still whistling the other one.

> REGNIER
> You forgot, eh? What about us? You think maybe we have forgotten how to hear?

> LABOUSSERE
> Excuse me, Sergeant. I did forget.

> REGNIER
> Good. Tomorrow night, maybe I forget and take you on the patrol. How would you like that?

> LABOUSSERE
> I did forget. But there are just two tunes on it. How do you expect me to always remember in all this?

He gestures—indicates the wall.

> REGNIER
> Bah—that music box! When you go home—I will tell you what you do. You take one grenade with you—you lift the lid of that music box, like this—

Regnier pantomimes with hand.

> REGNIER
> (continuing)
> You pull the pin of that grenade and drop it in and close the box like this—

Pantomime again.

> LABOUSSERE'S VOICE
> In my music box? Why, I have not even finished paying for it.

REGNIER

So much the better. Neither you nor the music box will be there when the man comes to collect. To bed with you.
He turns to the others.

REGNIER

That means all of you. Get on, now.
Regnier goes out. The men prepare for bed. The music box owner looks quite depressed. The others still watch him.

FIRST SOLDIER

When he goes on leave—just think of the female damage he will do, with that music box and those curls.

SECOND SOLDIER

—When he gets it paid for.

THIRD SOLDIER

But after he has done the female damage, they can come and take the music box, eh, Laboussere?

FIRST SOLDIER

It will not play but two tunes. He can't get but two women with it.

SECOND SOLDIER

But who wants more than two—who wants more than one.

FOURTH SOLDIER

Who wants one even—that's why I enlisted.
Laboussere turns on them, harried.

LABOUSSERE

You know nothing of music—nothing of love. You—you—
The corporal is carefully putting away the dominoes.

CORPORAL

Come—come—get into bed—and you others—you let him be. Do you want to get him started talking about his confounded music box all night? Some of us want to sleep a little even if you don't.

FIFTH SOLDIER

I can't sleep. It smells bad in here.

SECOND SOLDIER

Then tie one of Laboussere's socks around your face. Tie
one of your own around it.

They get into the bunks.

CORPORAL

All right, Grandonnet.

Grandonnet removes one boot and holds it poised, looking about.

GRANDONNET

Everybody ready?

FIFTH SOLDIER

I can't sleep in here. Hasn't anybody got some scent?

CORPORAL

We all have by now. Shut up! Go ahead, Grandonnet.

Grandonnet hurls boot and puts out the candle. Complete darkness. We hear the men turn in their bunks, and scratching. The
scratching is a steady sound.

FIFTH SOLDIER'S VOICE

I wish I had some scent.

ANOTHER VOICE

Aw—go to sleep. You would need five hundred francs'
worth to smell it in here.

Steady sound of scratching.

CUT TO:

58 THE TRENCH NIGHT

Steady flares. Very little firing. Delaage and Regnier making round
of sentries. They stop.

DELAAGE

So, you are going to take me on patrol with you tomorrow night?

REGNIER

Yes, sir.

                    DELAAGE

—Because Captain Morache doesn't think I know enough
about war.

Regnier says nothing.

                    DELAAGE
          (continuing)
That's what it is, isn't it? You have known him longer
than I have. Isn't that it?

                    REGNIER

You're young, sir, and he has been out a good while. Two
years now. They say he will be a colonel this time next
year if he lives.

                    DELAAGE

But a hard officer—a hard man to be under.

                    REGNIER

This is war, sir—we are not out here for fun.

                    DELAAGE

You are right, Sergeant. If I've got to soldier I want to do
it well. I want a hard man to teach me how.

                    REGNIER

You will have a company some day yourself, sir, if you
live.

                    DELAAGE

If I live. And I have a good man to learn under.

                    REGNIER

You have a good man, sir.

                    DELAAGE

But hard?

Regnier does not answer for a moment.

                    REGNIER

A good man, sir.

                    DELAAGE

You're right, Sergeant. A good man. Let's get on with
this, shall we?

They go on.

CUT TO:

59 DUGOUT COMPLETE DARKNESS
Snores. Sound of one man turning, wakeful. Suddenly we hear
the digging underneath. The mine. We hear a man sit suddenly
up in his bunk.

> VOICE
> Psst—Regnier—Sergeant!!

No answer, but the snoring. We hear the man get up. He strikes a
light to the candle. It is the fifth soldier. The one who wanted the
scent. He kneels to the floor and listens. Three or four other men
sit up in their bunks, watching him. He rises, wild faced. He is
about to shout when the other four jump down. At once the whole
dugout is awake, as the men kneel on the floor in turn and listen,
looking at one another with wild surmise.

> FIRST SOLDIER
> They are mining—under us!

> SECOND SOLDIER
> Get out of here—get out of here!

In a body they rush toward the stairs, fighting to reach the steps
as Regnier descends.

> REGNIER
> —'Shun! 'Shun! What the hell is this?

The men pause—glaring at him. The man who wanted scent
shrieks—

> SOLDIER
> Mining—under us!! They are going to blow us up!

The men are about to rush Regnier. He does not move—looking at
them.

> REGNIER
> Blow you up! Why not! What are you here for? What are
> they paying for a franc a day for?

> A SOLDIER
> But like rats in a hole!

REGNIER

Rats—hah!! So much the better. We can spare a few rats.
You there, Bixiou—call the lieutenant.

The corporal goes out.

VOICE

The lieutenant, mind you. Not the captain. Much he
cares if we—

REGNIER

'Shun—there—you!!
> (to the corporal)

Hurry!

Regnier looks at the men.

REGNIER

Ain't you ashamed—soldiers! Soldiers.

He descends. They make way for him. He too kneels and listens
at the floor, the men watching him. He looks up.

REGNIER

Suppose they find money under there. A pot of gold, eh?
Who should it belong to?

A SOLDIER

To us—to France—this is ours. Our line. We have held it
two years now. It should be ours.

REGNIER

And what would you do with it? Buy wine? You, Laboussere—you would pay for your music box first, I hope.

Enter Morache, Delaage, corporal. The men watch, breathless,
while Morache kneels and listens at the floor. Morache rises, looks
about at the faces watching him. He looks at Regnier.

MORACHE

Well, Sergeant?

REGNIER

They are afraid, sir—they want to get out.

MORACHE

And go where?

The men look at him.

MORACHE

Into the next dugout or the one beyond that? Don't you
know that when this dugout goes the other will go too.
Do you think the entire German army is just trying to
blow up the Fourth Platoon?

They look at him.

MORACHE

As long as you can hear the digging—there is no danger.
They are not going to blow up their own sappers. Get
back to bed.

Morache goes out. The men watch him. Then they surge forward
toward Delaage.

A SOLDIER

You are not like him. You won't let us die here like rats!

REGNIER

'Shun—'Shun! There!

The men halt—staring at Delaage.

DELAAGE

Now—what—didn't the captain tell you?

A SOLDIER

Will we have to stay here? Fifty hours down here—

CORPORAL

Not fifty hours—but forty-four now.

DELAAGE

You will stay here until you are relieved. It will not go as long as you can hear the digging.

LABOUSSERE

But must we stay awake to hear when they stop digging?

CORPORAL

Shut up, I tell you, fool. Didn't the captain and the lieutenant both tell you there is no danger yet?

A SOLDIER

But what about tomorrow? What then? Will the lieutenant get us out before it blows up?

REGNIER

Of course he will—enter your bunks now.

SOLDIER

But does he promise?

They look at Delaage.

DELAAGE

Yes—I promise. Enter your bunks now. Stand to, in three hours.

Delaage goes out.

CUT TO:

60 CAPTAIN'S DUGOUT NIGHT

Morache at table with papers. Two other officers are asleep in bunks. Enter Delaage. Morache does not look up at once. Delaage stops a little back from the table, looking at Morache.

DELAAGE

I promised them I would get them out before it goes.

Morache looks up.

MORACHE

How?

Delaage shrugs and moves toward table.

DELAAGE

Got a cigarette?

Morache gestures toward a tin box on the table and looks down at the papers. Delaage takes out a cigarette.

MORACHE

Suppose I evacuated my whole front. How long would it be before the Hun found it out? Then he wouldn't even need his mine. Somebody must be here. I hope it is not us. I wish it could be no one. But somebody must be here.

Delaage lights his cigarette. Morache is busy with the papers.

DELAAGE

So I am to go with Regnier on the patrol tomorrow night?

Morache does not look up.

MORACHE

Yes. You had better get some sleep. Wake Daguillette to relieve you.

Delaage does not move.

DELAAGE

To learn about the war.

Again Morache notices the overtone in his voice and looks up. They look at one another.

MORACHE

How long were you out before, Delaage? I mean at the front—not how long you have worn that stripe.

DELAAGE

I have never been in the front lines before.

MORACHE

I thought not. Wake Daguillette.

DELAAGE

Very good, Captain.

DISSOLVE TO:

61 DAWN BOMBARDMENT
Men standing along fire step. A man sitting on a box of ammunition, eating bread and drinking from a canteen. Daylight grows swiftly.

DISSOLVE TO:

62 FOURTH PLATOON DUGOUT   MORNING
Steady sound of digging underneath. The hand with the bayonet scratches out another section of marks on the wall. Only eight sections are left now.

VOICE

Forty hours more!

CAMERA MOVES BACK to see crowd around the man with the bayonet.

VOICE

Forty hours! And eight of us to draw a stake. That will be five hours apiece. I'll take the last five.

SECOND SOLDIER

No, you won't.

FIRST SOLDIER

Yes, I will. I spoke first. Didn't I, Bixiou?
The corporal turns. Lifts hand.

CORPORAL

Silence! Silence! I will declare the whole thing off.
The men get quiet.

CORPORAL

(continuing)
Now, we have eight sections at five hours each. We will number eight chances from one to eight and draw them. If the mine goes off during the first five hours, number one wins—if in the second, number two—

FIRST SOLDIER

But if he wins then—what good will it do him?

CORPORAL

You will not lose at least.

SOLDIER

But suppose it does not—then number eight will win it all. He will be the one who will spend the eight francs.

CORPORAL

Then you would not pay one franc to be out of here before it blows up?

Silence. The corporal looks about.

CORPORAL

As I was saying—if it does not blow up until we go out, we will all win. We will buy wine with the eight francs. Agreed?

ALL VOICES

Agreed.

The corporal takes from his pocket eight slips of paper and puts them into a helmet. A hand reaches in to draw. Voice in background.

VOICE

Mail—mail!

CUT TO:

63 INT DUGOUT MORNING

The men are receiving mail. Two or three get none, are disgruntled. Others grasp the letters eagerly. We see one man with a letter and a photograph of his wife and two children. We see a part of the letter. "Dear Michele: The cow has recovered. It was not serious. The children and I are well and we are crossing off the days on the calendar until your next leave is due."

PAN TO LABOUSSERE. He has a letter. His face expresses amazement and despair. We see this letter. "Monsieur Theodule Laboussere, Arles, France. *Please Forward*. We have not received any remittance on the music box bought by you in eight months. If this is not attended to at once, something of a very serious nature will happen to you in about sixty days from date. Yours very respectfully, Universal Collection Agency."

We see the corporal moving among the men with his helmet of lottery tickets.

> CORPORAL
>
> Come, come, draw if you intend to.

Men begin to draw again.

DISSOLVE TO:

64 SCRATCHES ON THE WALL
Hand with bayonet scratches out the sixth section, leaving only five.

> VOICE
>
> Now we have just twenty-five hours.

> ANOTHER VOICE
>
> Officer—'Shun!

THE CAMERA MOVES BACK. We see the men at attention as Delaage descends.

> DELAAGE
>
> At ease, men.

The men break attention. They resume their pursuits. The domino game—the man who received a letter from his wife, writing a letter.

> DELAAGE
>
> You have got through the night and now you have just one more.

> A SOLDIER
>
> Twenty-five hours, Lieutenant.

> DELAAGE
>
> Twenty-five hours then. As soon as it is dark tomorrow night, we go out. You can begin to get your gear together.

A babble of voices, happy and joyful. Delaage turns and is about to go back upstairs when he stops. All the men stop what they are doing in their various attitudes. We look from face to face. The wild expressions of horror and fear. Then we realize that the digging has stopped. We see the men playing dominoes stop, one with a domino suspended in his hand. We see the man writing the letter look up from it.

                                                                CUT TO:

65 INSERT LETTER

"My dear wife:

I'm pleased that the cow is well. The picture of you and the children makes me very homesick. I, too, am counting the days until my leave comes due."

HAND COMES INTO CAMERA and crumples letter.

CAMERA MOVES BACK. We see all the men about to make a break for the stairs. Delaage sees this too. He steps down. His movement toward them stops them all. They watch him wildly as he crosses quietly to the domino game, takes the domino from the man's hand and plays it. His voice is calm and quiet.

                          DELAAGE
            That's your next move, Grandonnet. See?
A babble of voices. Again the men are about to break for the stairs. Delaage's voice is sharp and stern now.

                          DELAAGE
            'Shun—'shun!
The men stop, staring at him.

                          DELAAGE
            Listen!
They realize that the digging has started again. The tension relaxes a little, though the men still watch him. We might see one man wiping the sweat from his face.

                          DELAAGE
        You see. We didn't get it then and we're not going to get
        it. Didn't I promise you? They just stopped for a minute.
        They just stopped to change shifts.

                          SOLDIER
            — or to drink some beer.
Laughter of relief as Delaage turns.

> DELAAGE
>
> Just stop thinking about it until you are in the estaminet tomorrow night. Carry on.

He goes out.

DISSOLVE TO:

66 SCRATCHES ON WALL

The hand with the bayonet drawing a line through another section.

> VOICE
>
> Now we just have fifteen hours.

DISSOLVE TO:

67 NO-MAN'S-LAND OUTSIDE THE FRENCH WIRE NIGHT

We see the gap in the wire. Regnier crawls out, followed by Delaage. Their faces are black. Delaage still has his gas mask slung around his neck. They crawl on. Each time a flare goes up they crouch, then crawl on again. Regnier looks back and sees Delaage's gas mask.

> REGNIER
>
> Why did you bring that, sir? Didn't you know you are not to wear anything that can hang in the wire?

> DELAAGE
>
> No. They didn't tell me. What shall I do with it? Carry it back?

> REGNIER
>
> Throw it away, sir. There won't be any gas out here tonight, with a west wind.

> DELAAGE
>
> What about that cloud of it down in the valley in front of the 153rd?

> REGNIER
>
> That's been there two days now. It won't get up here unless the wind changes, and then we'd get the alarm from the trenches.

> DELAAGE
>
> What sort of alarm? If it should begin to move, the Boche will attack, so the first alarm we'd get would be our own machine-gun barrage, wouldn't it? And then what?

Regnier shrugs.

> DELAAGE
> (continuing)
>
> Well, let's get on anyway. Before we go back into the wire, I'll throw it away.

They go on.

CUT TO:

68 FRENCH OUTPOST NIGHT

Excitement between the two observers.

> FIRST OBSERVER
>
> Look!

They see the gas cloud. One observer wets his finger and raises it to see where the wind is. They prepare to put on their gas masks. First observer catches up telephone.

> FIRST OBSERVER
> (into telephone)
>
> Gas coming in. . . . What, a patrol out? . . . All right.

He puts the phone down.

> FIRST OBSERVER
> (continuing)
>
> It's Regnier and Lieutenant Delaage. I hope Regnier will have sense enough to get them into a shell hole when the barrage starts.

They put on their gas masks and crouch in the hole, watching the gas cloud.

CUT TO:

69 NO-MAN'S-LAND NIGHT

Regnier has raised himself onto his arms. On his face is an expression of concern. He is sniffing. He rises to his feet. He obviously sees the gas cloud.

DELAAGE

What shall we do—run for it?

REGNIER

We can't. As soon as the outpost reports it, they will start the machine guns.

DELAAGE

Then we must just lie here and hope the wind changes. That it?

REGNIER

Yes, sir.

DELAAGE

Good. Here.

Regnier turns. Delaage extends the gas mask.

REGNIER

Put it on, sir—quick!

DELAAGE

Take it, Sergeant!

REGNIER

Me?

DELAAGE

Yes—take it.

REGNIER

No—no, sir! Put it on for God's sake! Can't you smell it?

DELAAGE

Sergeant!

They look at one another.

DELAAGE

(continuing)

Put it on.

REGNIER

No, sir.

Delaage holds out his arms and points to his stripe.

DELAAGE

My little stripe is smaller than your chevron—but it ranks
it. Put on the mask, Sergeant.

REGNIER

I won't, sir.

DELAAGE

Must I take my pistol to make you? Or shall I just report
you for insubordination when we get back?

Regnier takes the mask slowly.

REGNIER

It ain't the insubordination, sir—it ain't that. I—

DELAAGE

I know it's not. Put it on. The wind may change yet.

Regnier puts on the mask. They lie in a shell hole. Behind them
the machine guns begin.

CUT TO:

70   OBSERVATION POST

The two observers watching the gas cloud. One of them lifts his
mask, sniffs carefully. They both remove masks. The observer wets
his finger and raises it again to test the wind.

OBSERVER

(pantomime of speech not heard because of firing
of machine guns)

He takes up telephone and speaks into it in pantomime. The machine guns gradually cease.

DISSOLVE TO:

71   CAPTAIN'S DUGOUT

Morache sitting at table. Delaage and Regnier facing him. Regnier
is at attention.

MORACHE

So you insisted on Regnier taking the mask.

(Delaage says nothing; Morache turns to Regnier)
Well, Sergeant?

REGNIER

Yes, sir.

MORACHE

You are dismissed and relieved.
>   (Regnier salutes and goes out; Morache looks at
> Delaage)

So you did make him take the mask.

Delaage shrugs.

DELAAGE

Regnier is the best sergeant you've got—that my platoon has got, anyway. I don't think I'm the best officer. And even if I was, you can get plenty more officers, but sergeants like Regnier don't grow on trees, as I told you the other day—

MORACHE

Lieutenant Delaage—

Delaage looks at Morache, comes to attention and salutes. He sees something in Morache's face which causes him to hold the salute stiff at attention.

MORACHE

>   (continuing)

And as I told you the other day—I don't need replacement subalterns to tell me how to run my company. Do you understand?

Delaage says nothing. Stiff at salute. Morache looks at him.

MORACHE

>   (continuing)

You are a stout fellow, Delaage.
>   (he looks at Delaage, who does not move)

But you are a damned fool!

>   DISSOLVE:

72 MARKS ON THE DUGOUT WALL

The hand with the bayonet draws a heavy line through the last five marks.

>   DISSOLVE TO:

73 THE TRENCH NIGHT
The company is being relieved. The sentries step down from the fire step and are replaced. Men with packs moving down the trench, while other men with packs pass them. Same scene of jostling and orderly and quiet pandemonium as before. NCO speaking in his sharp, quiet voice.

CUT TO:

74 ANOTHER PART OF TRENCH
Morache and the relieving captain as the men pass them going out and coming in.

> RELIEVING CAPTAIN
> So I left you a wounded man on the wire and you leave me a mine to sit over.

> MORACHE
> I quieted your wounded man, though.

> RELIEVING CAPTAIN
> And I suppose I am to go down and explode your mine— is that it?

> MORACHE
> Well, I hope you don't have to. I hope you don't get it.

> RELIEVING CAPTAIN
> If I don't—you will when you come back in.

> MORACHE
> But I can still hope you don't get it, can't I?

> RELIEVING CAPTAIN
> Thanks.

They salute. Morache follows the last of his men down the trench.

CUT TO:

75 INSIDE OF COMMUNICATION TRENCH LOOKING OUT ON THE REGISTERED CORNER
Shells bursting at 30-second intervals as before. The trench is choked with men. Helmets, rifles, etc., in silhouette against the shell burst.

DELAAGE

All right, men. When I give the word, run for it. First
section ready?

NCO'S VOICE

First section ready, sir.

The shell burst comes.

DELAAGE'S VOICE

Run!

The first section crosses safely. The shell burst comes behind it.

DELAAGE'S VOICE

Second section ready?

NCO'S VOICE

Second section ready, sir.

The shell burst comes.

DELAAGE'S VOICE

Run!

The second section crosses. The shell burst comes behind it.

DELAAGE'S VOICE

(continuing)
Third section ready?

NCO'S VOICE

Third section ready, sir.

The shell burst comes.

DELAAGE'S VOICE

Run!

The third section crosses. The shell burst comes behind it.

DISSOLVE TO:

76 A ROAD NIGHT

The gunfire is a faint murmur in the distance. The sky is dark. The
troops move along, beginning to straggle again. Now we hear Laboussere begin to whistle his mournful off-key "Marseillaise"
which is interrupted by two or three savage voices.

VOICES

Shut up! SHUT UP!

LABOUSSERE'S VOICE
I forgot.

ANOTHER VOICE
If you've got to whistle—for God's sake whistle the other one.

FADE OUT:

FADE IN:

77 CLOSEUP PIANO KEYBOARD
A girl's hands are playing Chopin. They play slowly and painfully.

78 INT MONIQUE'S ROOM NIGHT MONIQUE AT PIANO
It is a cheap, little upright model, the kind that used to be known as "cottage." She leans toward the music and scowls every time she hits a sour note. From her face we see that she has finished one page and is starting another. She stops. An expression of disgust comes over her face and she slaps the keys. She takes the music book in her hands and holds out the page she had started to play.

79 CLOSEUP MUSIC BOOK
in Monique's hands. It is old and dog-eared. We see that about an inch-and-a-half has been torn from the top of the page Monique had started to play.

80 CLOSE SHOT MONIQUE
She throws the book down in rage and bursts into tears. She gets out her handkerchief and starts to have a good cry, when a little clock on the mantelpiece strikes nine. An expression of weariness comes over her face. She dries her tears, then goes over to a table, picks up her hat, and puts it on. She walks to the window and looks up at the sky.

81 SKY MONIQUE'S ANGLE
It is a cloudy night and looks as though it might rain.

82 MEDIUM CLOSE SHOT MONIQUE
She goes to the clothes press, gets out a raincoat and puts it on. There is a knock at the door to which she has her back turned. It is a knock with a special rhythm. She whirls around.

> MONIQUE

Paul!

83 ANGLE ON DOOR
It bursts open and there stands Morache, the stains of battle still on him. They rush into each other's arms.

84 TWO-SHOT
He hugs her to him.

> MORACHE

Oh, Monique, my sweet, my precious, I've missed you so.

He kisses her hungrily. She draws back and looks at him at arm's length.

> MONIQUE

Is it really you? I still don't believe it.

> MORACHE

Didn't I say just a short business trip?

> MONIQUE

Let me look at you. Oh, my dear.

She goes back into his arms. He picks her up, carries her to the piano stool and sits down with her on his knees.

> MORACHE

We're billeted about three kilos down the road at Doriot's farm.

> MONIQUE

(nodding)
I know the place.

> MORACHE

I had to see the men settled first or I'd have been here an hour ago.

> MONIQUE

(slipping an arm around his neck)
Did you have a terrible time at the front, darling?

A haunted look comes over his face.

MORACHE

We nearly did. The Boche was digging a mine under us.
The men heard the digging and wanted to get out. My
orders were to hold our sector at all costs. I had to keep
them there.

MONIQUE

But you got them out safely.

MORACHE

Yes, but it was only luck. Five minutes later the trench
was blown a mile high.

MONIQUE

Oh!

She hugs him to her.

MORACHE

Sometimes I think I'll go crazy out there—making those
men face death. And not able to show how *I* feel about
it. That's the worst—having to be cold and calm and im-
personal.
    (furiously)
What's the matter with them? Why can't they see? I'm
human. I don't enjoy it either. I'm afraid, too. More
afraid than all of 'em put together.

He is almost weeping. Monique holds him against her and strokes
his hair.

MONIQUE

My poor, tired darling! There, there. You'll have a nice
long rest now and forget it for a while.

He gives himself to her nearness for a long moment.

MORACHE

    (eyes closed)
Just holding you like this is making me forget already.
Just being able to touch you makes the misery melt away.

MONIQUE

    (touched)
My dear!

Morache raises his face and looks at her.

                    MORACHE
Oh, my precious, couldn't we . . . couldn't we have this
evening together?
Monique glances over his shoulder.

85 CLOSEUP CLOCK FACE
It says 9:10.

86 TWO-SHOT
Monique looks at him guiltily.

                    MONIQUE
You know I'd love it, darling, but I'm late now and the
head nurse has got it in for me.

                    MORACHE
            (sighing and nodding)
I suppose you're right. I've got to inspect the new
ammunition dump here and ought to be on the job
myself.
She slides off his lap. She smiles up at him.

                    MONIQUE
This terrible war!
Morache takes her in his arms and holds her cheek against his.

                    MORACHE
It's all right now. . . . When can I see you?

                    MONIQUE
I'll come to your billet at noon tomorrow.

                    MORACHE
That will be marvelous. . . . May I take you to the hospital?

                    MONIQUE
Oh, darling. I'm so late. It will be easier for us both if we
say au revoir right here.

                    MORACHE
My precious!
They kiss.
                                    DISSOLVE TO:

87 MEDIUM CLOSE SHOT   UNDER WING OF GERMAN PLANE
NIGHT
showing the Maltese Cross painted on it. Noise of motor on sound
track.

88 MEDIUM LONG SHOT   BOMBING SQUADRON OF GERMAN
PLANES IN FORMATION   NIGHT

89 MEDIUM CLOSE SHOT   COCKPIT GERMAN PLANE   NIGHT
showing the observer pointing downward as the pilot nods.

90 AERIAL SHOT   VILLAGE   NIGHT
showing the village lights shining.

91 CLOSE SHOT   BOMB RELEASE LEVER   INT   GERMAN
COCKPIT   NIGHT
A hand pulls the lever.

92 CLOSE SHOT   BOMBING MECHANISM UNDER PLANE
showing a pair of bombs taking off for the village below.

93 MEDIUM CLOSE TRUCK SHOT   NIGHT
Monique is walking along a deserted street when suddenly on the
sound track there is the noise of a terrific explosion, followed immediately by another. She reacts and runs for cover against a wall.

94 MEDIUM LONG SHOT   VILLAGE STREET   NIGHT
A motorcycle ridden by a French soldier blowing a siren whizzes
toward the CAMERA, followed by a fire truck. The street lights
wink out rapidly one by one. Merchants begin closing the shutters
on their shop fronts. Small groups of soldiers and civilians rush
about seeking cover.

95 MEDIUM SHOT ANTI-AIRCRAFT GUN NIGHT
Mounted on a truck with several big searchlights, it blazes up to
the heavens.

96 MEDIUM SHOT   SQUADRON OF GERMAN PLANES   NIGHT

97 MEDIUM CLOSE SHOT   SQUADRON LEADER IN COCKPIT
NIGHT
He looks to the right and gives an arm signal.

98 MEDIUM SHOT   FORMATION GERMAN PLANES   NIGHT
The plane on the end dives.

99 MEDIUM LONG SHOT FRENCH FLYING FIELD NIGHT
Several fighting planes are being hastily wheeled out of their hangars.

100 TWO-SHOT NIGHT
A squadron commander is shouting over the noise of idling motors to one of his aviators.

> SQUADRON COMMANDER
> They're trying to bomb the ammunition dumps.

On the sound track is heard the roar of a propeller. The explosion of bombs is heard on the sound track.

101 INT CELLAR NIGHT
The room is lit by faint candle light. On the sound track are heard the strains of "Ach Du Lieber Augustine" gaily rendered.

CAMERA PANS slowly around the cellar, picking out a couple of busted-down sofas, rickety chairs, dusty paintings, piles of draperies and other superannuated household furnishings, and finally stops on a harpsichord which is being played by Delaage. He has taken off his tunic and is in his shirtsleeves.

On one side of the harpsichord is a candle in a saucer; on the other, a bottle of cognac from which he takes a long pull every now and then. Directly above him is the cellar window giving onto the street. The ceiling of the cellar is so low that when Delaage stands up he has to duck his head.

On the sound track is heard the explosion of another pair of bombs. Delaage fits the tempo of "Ach Du Lieber Augustine" to the detonation of the bombs. He will play a few bars, stop, take a drink, waiting for more explosions. When they come, he takes up the tune again. From his face we can see that he is enjoying himself hugely. He has picked up the bottle, raised it to his lips, and is just starting to drink when he suddenly notices something.

102 CLOSE SHOT CELLAR WINDOW DELAAGE'S ANGLE
A skirt and a trim pair of ankles are seen on the other side of the window. Bomb explosions are heard on the sound track.

103 MEDIUM CLOSE SHOT DELAAGE
He puts down the bottle, jumps up, bumps his head, then opens the cellar window, which swings back from the top.

104 MEDIUM CLOSE SHOT EXT HOUSE NIGHT MONIQUE
cowering against the wall of the house. She screams, looks down.
A hand has a hold on one of her ankles. She pulls away in alarm.
A couple of bombs explode off scene.

>   DELAAGE'S VOICE
> Want to get blown up? Come down here—around the
> back.

                                        QUICK DISSOLVE TO:

105 INT   CELLAR NIGHT
Delaage is playing "Ach Du Lieber Augustine" again, and nipping
from his bottle. He is a little drunk. There is a knock at the door.
He jumps up, bumps his head again, and goes to the door, taking
the bottle with him. He puts his hand on the knob.

>   DELAAGE
>   (melodramatically)
>   Open Sesame!

He pulls the door back and is in the middle of a deep bend when
he notices Monique.

>   DELAAGE
>   (exuberantly)
>   My aunt's pen holder!

Monique, alarmed at the sight of him, hesitates, but a couple more
bombs explode outside and she comes in. Delaage takes her by the
arm.

>   DELAAGE
> What a delightful surprise! Welcome to these marbled
> halls.

Monique looks around her curiously. Delaage gestures floridly at
one of the busted-down sofas.

>   DELAAGE
>   (continuing)
>   Recline upon our silken ottomans!

He waves his bottle.

>   DELAAGE
>   (continuing)

Sip the wines of our country!
He presses the bottle on her.

DELAAGE

(continuing)
Trod from the grape by the feet of milk-white virgins!
He bumps his head. Monique giggles in spite of herself.

DELAAGE

(continuing)
Cognac—I stole it from the mess sergeant.
He hands her the bottle.

DELAAGE

(continuing)
And I shall play you a piece especially composed for this
occasion.
He sits down at the harpsichord and begins to play "Ach Du Lieber Augustine." Bombs burst outside.

DISSOLVE TO:

106 MEDIUM LONG SHOT FRENCH PURSUIT SQUADRON IN
FORMATION NIGHT
The planes tear along heading for the enemy.

107 CLOSE SHOT BOMBING MECHANISM
Another pair of bombs takes off for the village. A few seconds later
there is a detonation from below.

108 MEDIUM CLOSE SHOT INT COCKPIT GERMAN BOMBER
NIGHT
The observer taps the pilot on the shoulder and points off.

109 LONG SHOT FRENCH PURSUIT SQUADRON NIGHT
showing the French planes drawing nearer at a rapid rate.

110 LONG SHOT GERMAN BOMBING SQUADRON NIGHT
turning and starting for the German lines.

111 INT CELLAR NIGHT CLOSE SHOT HARPSICHORD
Monique leans on the instrument, fascinated. Delaage is just fin-
ishing the closing bars of a Chopin piece.

MONIQUE
Oh, thank you so much. That was heavenly.—Can you play the E-flat Nocturne?

DELAAGE
(looking at her appraisingly)
Nothing easier.
He takes up the bottle and has a long drink.

DELAAGE
(continuing)
Nothing like brandy for an E-flat Nocturne.
He falls to and plays it beautifully. It is the piece Monique was trying to play on her cottage piano. Monique, entranced by the music, looks at his face. He looks up from the keyboard, sees her, and smiles. She smiles back.

DISSOLVE TO:

112   MEDIUM LONG SHOT   AIR BATTLE   NIGHT
Two French pursuit planes are swarming around a German bomber like wasps attacking a clumsy animal.

113   MEDIUM SHOT   COCKPIT OF FRENCH PLANE
showing the machine gun in action.

114   CLOSE SHOT   MACHINE GUN
in action.

115   MEDIUM SHOT   COCKPIT GERMAN PLANE
showing the pilot falling back from the controls, wounded.

116   LONG SHOT   GERMAN PLANE
falling in flames.

DISSOLVE TO:

117   INT   CELLAR   MEDIUM CLOSE SHOT ON HARPSICHORD
Monique is struggling in Delaage's arms. He is pretty drunk.

DELAAGE
Yes, Yes! Come on.

MONIQUE
No, no. I must go. The raid's over.

Delaage again tries to kiss her. She turns her face away. Suddenly the noise of rain is heard on the sound track. Both look up at the window. Delaage bursts out laughing.

> DELAAGE
>
> Aha! I'm a real villain. I had the rain turned on.

He blows out the candle, leaving the room lit only by the glow from the hearth fire.

118 CLOSE SHOT CELLAR WINDOW THEIR ANGLE
showing the rain falling very hard outside.

118A TWO-SHOT

> DELAAGE
>
> (coaxing)
> Ah, come on now. Be a nice girl.

> MONIQUE
>
> (struggling)
> That's just what I'm going to be.

She breaks from his grasp.

119 MEDIUM SHOT INT CELLAR
She runs for the door, but Delaage heads her off and spreads his arms in front of it.

> DELAAGE
>
> (scowling)
> So that's it, eh? 'Fore you'd be dishonored, you'd die of pneumonia.

> MONIQUE
>
> Please let me go.

> DELAAGE
>
> I'll let you go.

He rushes at her, seizes her, lifts her bodily off the floor, and whirls her around. Monique screams. He takes her over and dumps her on the broken-down sofa. He glowers at her.

> DELAAGE
>
> I'll show you!

He dashes over to the pile of draperies, picks up an armful, and throws them on her.

DELAAGE
(thickly)
Here! Keep your virtue warm!

He goes back to the pile of draperies again and seizes a piece of stuff that looks as though it were part of an old cozy-corner. It is fastened by rings to a pole with a spearhead. He whips the rings off the pole, kicks the hanging into the corner, and lays the spearhead between the two sofas. All this time he has been bumping his head on the ceiling. He points down at the spear.

DELAAGE
There! A sword between us!

Monique giggles.

DELAAGE
(angrily)
Oh! A sword isn't enough, eh?

He goes over to his tunic and overcoat, fishes his service pistol out of his holster, and hands it to her.

DELAAGE
There! And see that you sell it dearly!

He goes to the pile of draperies, gathers up an armful, walks over to his sofa, and proceeds to cover himself up. He turns his back to Monique. Monique looks at him, smiling.

MONIQUE
You needn't be like this.

Delaage lifts his head and glares at her over his shoulder.

DELAAGE
Got plenty of bullets for your honor?

He lies down and turns his back to her grouchily.

MONIQUE
Yes, thank you. Good night.

Delaage does not look around.

DELAAGE
Good night!

DISSOLVE TO:

120 INT CELLAR DAY CLOSE SHOT DELAAGE
Delaage wakes up and from his facial contortions we see that he has a head. He gets up on his elbows and notices a piece of paper on his chest. He picks it up and looks at it.

121 CLOSEUP SHEET OF MUSIC
ripped from the tattered music book that was on the harpsichord. The piece is "Goodbye Forever" by Tosti. A circle has been drawn around the title with a burnt stick. Beside it is a message: "Thanks for saving me from boredom, pneumonia, and dishonor. Pen Holder."

122 MEDIUM CLOSE SHOT DELAAGE
He looks over at the other sofa.

123 CLOSE SHOT SOFA
It is empty.

124 CLOSE SHOT DELAAGE
He crumples up the message and hurls it from him furiously.

DISSOLVE TO:

125 COURTYARD EXT FARMHOUSE
This is a different one from the previous one. Soldiers sit about in various attitudes cleaning themselves and their gear.

QUICK DISSOLVE TO:

126 MORACHE'S ORDERLY ROOM INT FARMHOUSE
Morache is at his desk listening to Delaage, who is standing in front of the desk.

> DELAAGE
> My luck's not been very good so far. I met a gorgeous one last night, but got nowhere at all.

> MORACHE
> (chuckling)
> Well, Delaage, never say die. You have the tradition of the company to keep up.

DELAAGE
(grinning)
I'll do my best, sir.
There is a knock at the door.

MORACHE
Yes?

127 MEDIUM CLOSE SHOT DOOR
Monique enters. She is wearing a nurse's uniform. She looks up
and reacts.

128 FLASH HEAD CLOSEUP DELAAGE
reacting.

129 MEDIUM SHOT INT ORDERLY ROOM
Morache rises and crosses to Monique.

MORACHE
Darling!
He kisses her on both cheeks. Then he takes her by the arm and
starts leading her back toward the desk.

MORACHE
Did you get caught in that raid last night?
They have come up to where Delaage is standing. Monique looks
at Delaage.

MONIQUE
Yes, but I was all right.

MORACHE
This is Lieutenant Delaage. Lieutenant, this is Mademoiselle Achard.

DELAAGE
(saluting)
Enchanted to make your acquaintance, Mademoiselle.
They shake hands. Monique says nothing. There is a knock at the
door.

MORACHE
Yes?

130 MEDIUM CLOSE SHOT DOOR
Bouffiou comes in and salutes.

> BOUFFIOU
>
> Major Dupin would like to see you a moment, sir.

131 MEDIUM SHOT GROUP

> MORACHE
>
> Tell him right away. . . .
> (to others)
> Excuse me a moment, please.

He goes out of the shot. The sound of the door closing is heard on the sound track. Delaage turns to Monique.

> DELAAGE
>
> Mademoisell Achard, as I said before, I am enchanted to make your acquaintance.

Monique looks at him helplessly.

> DELAAGE
>
> (continuing)
> If you will give me the address I shall be honored to visit your salon.

> MONIQUE
>
> (pleading)
> Please—we must never see each other again. I mean it.

> DELAAGE
>
> Nonsense. What's the address?

> MONIQUE
>
> I won't tell you.

> DELAAGE
>
> Well, Mademoiselle, you will force me to turn detective. You know you're not exactly dressed as a scrubwoman.

> MONIQUE
>
> I don't ever want to see you.

> DELAAGE
>
> Why, of course you do. Don't you know musical comedy?

It's the lieutenant, not the captain, who always gets the
girl.

He twirls an imaginary moustache. Morache enters, and goes up
to them.

> MORACHE
> (to Monique)
> How about some lunch?
> (to Delaage)
> That'll be all, Lieutenant.

Delaage looks at them both.

> DELAAGE
> Are you sure, sir?

> MORACHE
> (puzzled)
> Certainly.

> DELAAGE
> (saluting)
> Very good, sir.

FADE OUT:

FADE IN:

132 INT HOSPITAL WARD
Delaage walks rapidly through the ward looking to the right and
left at the nurses.

DISSOLVE TO:

133 INT ANOTHER WARD
showing Delaage looking at more nurses.

DISSOLVE TO:

134 INT HALLWAY DAY
Delaage comes up the hallway, peeking in doors until finally he
stops at one.

135 MEDIUM CLOSE SHOT DOOR OF HOSPITAL ROOM DAY
DELAAGE'S ANGLE
showing a screen before the bed. The top of a nurse's headdress
can be seen over the screen. Delaage tiptoes into the room.

136 MEDIUM CLOSE SHOT INT HOSPITAL ROOM DAY
On the other side of the screen Monique is making the bed. Delaage's head peeks around the screen and he sees her. He comes
around himself and tickles her in the ribs as she is bending over.
She gives a little shriek and whirls around. He seizes her in his
arms and lifts her off the floor.

137 TWO-SHOT
Their conversation is conducted in whispers. Delaage is trying to
kiss her and she is struggling.

> MONIQUE
> No, no! You mustn't! Somebody will see us.

> DELAAGE
> Yes, yes! Come on now.

> MONIQUE
> No, no. We aren't allowed even to speak to officers.
Delaage tries again to kiss her.

> DELAAGE
> Never mind the speaking!
She ducks out of his arms and runs to the door.

138 MEDIUM CLOSE SHOT DOOR
Monique shoots a quick look down the hall and reacts.

139 MEDIUM LONG SHOT MONIQUE'S ANGLE MEDICAL
STAFF
The head surgeon and nurses of the hospital are piloting a fat general and a lady in an ostrich-feather hat down the hall. The group
stops to talk to a wounded soldier in a wheelchair.

140 MEDIUM SHOT INT HOSPITAL ROOM
Delaage is sitting on the bed still grinning when Monique dashes
around the screen wringing her hands.

> MONIQUE
> The staff is coming! With a general! The head nurse will
> see us! What'll we do?
Delaage looks around wildly. The braying laugh of the general can
be heard on the sound track, and the approach of heavily shod
feet on the corridor linoleum.

MONIQUE
(in agony)
Oh!

Delaage whips off his cap and tunic, flings them into the cup-
board, and with a bound leaps into the bed and pulls the covers
up to his ears, turning his back to the door.

The screen is moved aside by the head nurse. The general, the
general's wife, and rest of the group come in. Monique looks at
them apprehensively. The visitors survey the room.

GENERAL'S WIFE
What a pretty room.

141 MEDIUM SHOT GROUP
standing around Delaage's bed.

GENERAL'S WIFE
And what is the matter with this poor man?
All look inquiringly at Monique.

MONIQUE
(stuttering)
Oh—uh—uh—

The head surgeon goes to the foot of the bed and picks up the
fever chart which is hanging fastened there.

142 CLOSEUP DELAAGE
reacting in alarm to the question.

HEAD SURGEON'S VOICE
(chuckling)
This seems to be a case of mumps.
Delaage takes it big.

HEAD SURGEON'S VOICE
Well, old man, and how do we feel today?

143 MEDIUM CLOSE SHOT GROUP AROUND BED
Delaage turns over and faces them. He has blown out his cheeks.
With an agonized look on his face, he points to his swollen jowls.

GENERAL'S WIFE
Poor boy! I'll send him some gruel as soon as he can
swallow.

Delaage nods gratefully, and turns his back to them.

144 MEDIUM SHOT INT HOSPITAL ROOM
The visitors turn and go. Monique closes the door behind them.

145 CLOSE SHOT DELAAGE
He lets the air blow out of his cheeks in relief. He turns and sees
Monique bending over him. They roar with silent laughter.

146 TWO-SHOT
Delaage sits up in bed and seizes Monique in his arms.

> MONIQUE

No! No!

> DELAAGE

Yes! Why not?

> MONIQUE

On account of Paul.

> DELAAGE

Who? Morache? Never mind him. I'll go to him and have
it out.

> MONIQUE

Oh, no! You mustn't! You mustn't!

> DELAAGE

Why not? This isn't captain and lieutenant, it's man to
man.

> MONIQUE
> (in terror)

Oh, please, please never say anything to him about me.

> DELAAGE

But why not?

> MONIQUE

It isn't right. It isn't fair. He's been so fine to me.

> DELAAGE
> (laughing)

All right, if you say so.
He struggles to kiss her. She struggles back, but is weakening.

> MONIQUE
> You mustn't do this. It's crazy. There can't ever be any-
> thing between us.

> DELAAGE
> Yes there can. And there's going to be.

He takes her in his arms and kisses her. She returns the kiss in
spite of herself.

> DISSOLVE OUT:

147 INT MONIQUE'S ROOM NIGHT
Delaage is at the piano playing Chopin. Monique is leaning on the
piano watching him. He looks up at her and smiles gently. She
gives him a tender smile in return. He looks back at the music,
stops, and takes the music book off the rack.

148 CLOSEUP MUSIC BOOK
Delaage's hand holds out the torn page we saw before when Monique was playing.

149 MEDIUM CLOSE SHOT PIANO

> DELAAGE
> No wonder you can't play this piece, darling. I'll write it
> in for you.

He reaches in his pocket and pulls out a pencil.

150 CLOSEUP MUSIC BOOK
in Delaage's hand. With the rooster-top pencil he writes in the
missing score on the top of the next page.

151 TWO-SHOT NIGHT
Delaage puts the pencil on the music ledge and goes on playing.
He finishes the piece and turns to Monique. Monique looks off.

152 CLOSEUP CLOCK
It says a quarter to nine.

153 TWO-SHOT

> MONIQUE
> Darling, he's coming at nine. Please go.

DELAAGE
Won't you let me stay and settle it with him?

MONIQUE
Pierre, we've discussed all that. Please.

DELAAGE
(gently)
All right.

He rises, kisses her tenderly, takes up his cap, and goes. Monique sits at the piano stool and touches a key. She sees Delaage's pencil and takes it up. She looks at it, then she rises, goes over to the mantelpiece, and leans on it with her elbows. She looks at the clock, then at the pencil, then back at the clock again.

FADE OUT:

FADE IN:

154 Afternoon in the orderly room. A pair of heavy feet in army shoes crossed upon the table. A voice speaking in an assured, slightly patronizing tone.

BOUFFIOU
Certainly it's an attack. Do you know how many replacements we are going to get? Sixty-four—sixty-four replacements!

FIRST SOLDIER
Go on—I don't believe you.

CAMERA MOVING BACK. We see Bouffiou's head now as he sits with his feet on the desk, with three other soldiers standing about listening to him. Bouffiou might be the captain, or even the regimental commander himself as he sits and talks. We know that there are no officers about and that Bouffiou is one of those desk soldiers which you find in any regiment anywhere under the sun—unreliable, a braggart, probably a coward—good only to perform certain simple duties as long as there is someone there to see that he does it.

BOUFFIOU
Do you wish to see the order?

The others say nothing. It is apparent that they believe him, that he might and should know the truth, yet they know him of long to be a liar. He removes his feet from the desk, takes from his pocket his spectacle case, removes the glasses and closes the case and returns it to his pocket. He takes out another case, removes from it a small piece of chamois, wipes the spectacles, and returns the chamois to its case and the case to his pocket. Puts on the spectacles, shuffles through three or four papers on the desk, takes one up and peers at it until the first soldier takes it from his hand. The soldier reads it haltingly.

> FIRST SOLDIER
>
> From Transport Officer, Twelfth Army Supply Depot, to Officer Commanding Sixth Grenadier Company, 139th Infantry Regiment. You will at once acknowledge receipt of and report disposition of eight camels issued from Field Supply Depot, Twelfth Army, Bir-El Asab, Africa. January 12, 1892. Signed: Charles Moran, Major

Before the soldier finishes reading it—

> SECOND SOLDIER
>
> Phoo—that's no attack! If we had eight camels, we would eat them.

> BOUFFIOU
>
> All right—wait and see! Only just remember what I told you. In about three days from now, when we are climbing out of that trench with the whole Boche army shooting at us.

> SECOND SOLDIER
>
> We—we—the Boche that ever got close enough to you to shoot at you would need a passport.

> FIRST SOLDIER
>
> Wait! Is it the truth? Are we going to attack?

Bouffiou looks at them and shrugs.

> BOUFFIOU
>
> You don't have to believe me, but why should the whole regiment be built 20 percent overstrength—sixty-four replacements to this company? But wait and see if you had—

He turns his head. His expression changes. He springs to attention.

>   BOUFFIOU
>   'Shun!

They all stand at attention as Daguillette passes and goes on into the office. The men relax.

>   BOUFFIOU
>   (continuing)
>   Ask him if you don't believe me.

>   FIRST SOLDIER
>   You ask him—you are the orderly.

>   BOUFFIOU
>   Why should I ask him? It's not me that thinks I'm lying.
>   Listen, there are the trucks.

>   CUT TO:

155   COURTYARD DAYTIME
A LONG SHOT across the courtyard. Men resting, talking, smoking, cleaning equipment. Through the gate to the road with trucks loaded with replacements coming up.

CAMERA TRUCKS ACROSS COURTYARD. We see that the gate is ragged and jagged where old shells once struck it. We hear the voices of the soldiers.

>   FIRST VOICE
>   Here they come! Here come some more soldiers. Good!

>   SECOND VOICE
>   Why do you say good?

>   FIRST VOICE
>   More soldiers are always good.

CAMERA PASSES OUT GATE

156   REVERSE SHOT BACK THROUGH GATE FROM ACROSS ROAD
as the first truck comes up and stops and unloads and moves on.

The next truck comes up and stops and the men get out of it.

157 DOUBLE EXPOSURE, MAKING TRUCKS ALMOST
TRANSPARENT
We still see them unloading and the men getting out and entering
the courtyard. The jagged gate begins to take on the semblance of
a gaping and snaggled-tooth face which the men are entering.

> VOICE
> Look at that one! The Boche will lose his morning's sau-
> sage when he sees that one.

Laughter begins. A loud evil laughter as though the face were
laughing. More and more trucks come up and unload and more
and more men crowd through the gate, which is now definitely an
evil face. The laughter is harsh, and steady and loud.

DOUBLE EXPOSURE BEGINS TO FADE AS CAMERA COMES BACK
THROUGH GATE

Laughter dies away. We now see the replacements lined up. Their
packs and rifles at their feet. The veterans have scarcely looked
up at them. They are still engaged in their former pursuits, though
a few of them have approached as the corporal begins to call the
roll.

> CORPORAL
> Grignot!

> VOICE
> Here!

> CORPORAL
> Boutaville!

> VOICE
> Here!

> CORPORAL
> Brix!

> VOICE
> Here!

> CORPORAL
> Riviere!

VOICE

Here!

CORPORAL

Berthelot!

VOICE

Here!

THE CAMERA PASSES from face to face as the corporal calls the names. It outdistances his voice, so that it grows faint. THE CAMERA PAUSES for a second on an old man who is stiff at attention—a little ludicrously so. THE CAMERA SWINGS BACK UP the line of faces—FASTER NOW. We hear the corporal's voice again.

CORPORAL

Dimont!

VOICE

Here!

CORPORAL

All right, men! Stand easy but don't dismiss. You can smoke.

The corporal turns away. THE CAMERA SWINGS BACK along the line of faces. A babble of voices. The veterans come up and receive cigarettes from the replacements. Pantomime of various conversations as the CAMERA SWINGS AROUND. We hear a loud burst of laughter ahead of the camera, then a voice.

VOICE

Now, grandpa—you don't mean that!

An old man's voice, cracked and shrill.

OLD MAN'S VOICE

War! You call this war!

THE CAMERA PICKS UP THE GROUP. The old man who stood so stiffly at attention before is surrounded by veterans. We see that he is old, that he has dyed his hair and that the dye is now fading.

OLD MAN

Lying in a hole in the mud day after day and never seeing an enemy. Where's your cavalry charges? Where's your

flags to lead them and your bugles to blow them? War!
Bah!

FIRST SOLDIER

What do you know about war?

OLD MAN

Me! You ask me? Who faced an Uhlan charge and saw
the French Cuirassiers at—

SECOND SOLDIER

He was at Austerlitz. It's Marshal Ney in disguise.

OLD MAN

Not Austerlitz—but I was at—
He cuts himself short. He looks about at them, watches them almost cunningly. They are laughing at him.

SECOND SOLDIER

Now, grandpa, you know you ain't that old—you don't
look it. That hair looks almost natural enough to be a
wig.

OLD MAN

Never mind about that. I know this is not war, because I
was there. I blew a charge. I was just fourteen—but I
blew a charge. I can prove it. I have the bugle right here
in my pack—
Enter Regnier. The men give back a little. Regnier looks at the old
man.

REGNIER

What's this? You there? What is your name?
The old man turns, sees Regnier, comes to his stiff attention,
makes his florid, old-fashioned salute.

REGNIER

(continuing)
Don't salute me.
Third soldier moves forward.

THIRD SOLDIER

Salute me then.
The old man turns his salute toward the soldier.

OLD MAN

I will salute any soldier of France.

The soldier returns burlesque salute. Regnier watches grimly. He turns to the old man.

REGNIER

What's your name, I say?

OLD MAN

Marain, Sergeant.

REGNIER

Want to be a soldier, eh?

OLD MAN

(proudly)

I wish to serve France in the Fifth Company of the Thirty-ninth, Sergeant.

REGNIER

Hah! You can start now, then.

Regnier steps back, raises his voice.

REGNIER

Parade, 'shun! Captain Morache!

The replacements come to attention. We see the old man proud and stiff. As the CAMERA SWINGS BACK to pick up the door to the post of command, as Morache comes out and walks toward camera, is met by Regnier, who salutes him. Morache returns the salute.

MORACHE

At ease, men!

He looks swiftly along the line of faces.

MORACHE

You are now members of the Grenadier Company of the Second Battalion of the Thirty-ninth Regiment of the Line. This regiment was created by General Bonaparte. It came out of Waterloo with a good record. It has served in Indo-China and in Africa. It has been on this front as a combat unit since November 1914. It has not damaged that record yet. I do not expect any single man or any platoon or even this entire company to add stature to that record—but I do and will require that no man in it detract from that—

He stops. We see his gaze fixed up on something beyond the camera. We follow it and see the old man, stiff at attention, with something in his face even more than pride.

He is not smiling. He is quite grave. His face is just alight. CAMERA GOES BACK TO MORACHE. He is still looking at the old man. He has paused so long that we see Regnier looking at him curiously. Morache breaks his glance. His voice continues in the same tone.

> MORACHE
> —from it. That's all! You will be assigned to platoons at once.

He turns to Regnier.

> Come with me, Regnier.

He and Regnier return across the courtyard toward the post of command. The CAMERA SWINGS BACK, PASSES ALONG THE REPLACEMENTS at ease now, talking again, and comes to the old man. He has not moved. He still stands at attention, with that exalted expression on his face. The men around him are all looking at him.

> SOLDIER
> All right—grandpa—he's gone. You can take the ramrod out of your pants now.

The old man wakes up, breaks attention. Several veterans come up to him.

> OLD MAN
> And this is another thing you don't know. How to stand to attention when an officer speaks to you.

> FIRST SOLDIER
> That's because we don't have the officers you had at Waterloo, grandpa.

> SECOND SOLDIER
> Maybe Morache will make you captain in his place and you can show us.

THIRD SOLDIER

With that fish horn he says he's got, they will make him
a general at least.

OLD MAN

Fish horn—look!

He takes from his pack an old battered bugle. The men look at it.

OLD MAN

This fish horn as you call it blew the finest cavalry brigade in the world across the Meuse River one day—even
if we did lose. You were not there. You don't know. It's
not your fault that war has changed and become a matter
of hiding in holes with never an enemy's face to see—

Enter Regnier. He stares again at the old man and at the bugle. He
touches the old man's shoulder.

REGNIER

Come! Put that up. The captain wants you.

SECOND SOLDIER

My God, they're going to make him captain before supper time.

The old man puts the bugle back in his pack. His face is bright,
calm, serene.

OLD MAN

What if they do? Didn't France so honor a young girl,
once? And did France regret it?

He follows Regnier out.

CUT TO:

158 POST OF COMMAND INT CAPTAIN'S OFFICE
Morache behind the desk. Regnier and the old man facing him.
The old man at his stiff salute. The same exalted expression on his
face. Morache looks at him.

MORACHE

Go out a minute, Sergeant, will you?

Regnier goes out. Morache rises. Looking at the old man.

MORACHE

Father—!

The old man breaks salute. Runs forward. He and Morache embrace.

> OLD MAN
>
> My boy! My son!

> MORACHE
>
> What are you doing here?

> OLD MAN
>
> I've come to serve France. Oh, they tried to stop me—they would have made me a clerk—I, who at fourteen blew charges at the Sambre and at the Meuse. But it was simple. A few lies—a word here—a word there—and this—
>
> > (indicates his dyed hair)
>
> and lo! I am a member of the Grenadier Company of the Thirty-ninth. My son's company. Tell me, don't I look young enough. Would you take me to be a man of almost sixty—eh?

He is laughing, beaming. He looks at Morache's grim, cold, forbidding face. He stops. Steps back. Still staring at Morache.

> OLD MAN

Paul.

Morache just stares at him. The old man becomes calm.

> OLD MAN

So—you intend to send me back.

> MORACHE

Yes. This is no place for you.

> OLD MAN

So—the captain of the gallant Fifth Company of the Thirty-ninth would sacrifice France by removing a soldier from her armies just because that soldier happens to be kin to him—

He stares at Morache. After a moment—

> OLD MAN

Paul. Is it because you are afraid, not for me but of me?
> (he becomes excited again)
I am strong—hale. I am—

Morache just stares at him. The old man now draws himself up.

> OLD MAN

I am your father. You are a grown man—you hold a commission. Nevertheless I am still your father. I command you to let me remain.

Morache says nothing. The old man approaches. Lays his hands on Morache's shoulder—stares into his face.

> OLD MAN

Hah! Still adamant, eh? Good, then. Listen! I defy you! I will tell them that I who have been passed as fit for service have been refused admittance to my company because the captain of it does not wish his father to risk that danger to which he does not hesitate to send—

> MORACHE

Private Marain!

The old man looks at him. Comes to attention and salutes.

> MORACHE

Regnier!

Regnier enters.

> MORACHE

I want a runner to Brigade at once. You will ask for an order to evacuate Private Marain today. Reason, unfit for military service because of age. Charges, misrepresentation and perjury.

> REGNIER

Very good, sir.

He turns to go out.

> MORACHE

Wait!

Regnier halts and turns.

This is my father, Sergeant. Will you see that he has some supper before he goes back?

Regnier looks curiously at the old man.

CUT TO:

159 THE OLD MAN'S FACE—

At attention and salute. Tears running down. Regnier puts his hand on the old man's shoulder.

> REGNIER

Come, sir. I have some good tobacco in my quarters. Maybe a glass of wine.

They go out. Morache stares at the door a moment, then he sits at the table again and picks up the papers.

CUT TO:

160 STREET CORNER AFTERNOON

Café. Patron standing in front of it as an MP passes.

> PATRON

How goes it, soldier?

> MP

All right.

He is about to pass on.

PATRON

But maybe not so good tomorrow, eh?

The MP stops, look at him.

MP

Why tomorrow?

PATRON

(shrugs)

There are some in this village who will not be here tomorrow. Maybe they will not be at all tomorrow.

MP

What do you know about tomorrow?

PATRON

About the attack. I—I'm no general.

MP

But all the other old men and women and children in France seem to be. Who the hell told you anything about an attack?

PATRON

Whoever does? Perhaps a little bird.

MP

And perhaps that same little bird told the whole village, eh? Perhaps it has even told the Boche, eh? Perhaps it is a parrot, eh?

PATRON

Who knows? I'm no general. I know nothing about fighting wars.

The MP glares at him for a minute and goes on.

CUT TO:

161 INT SMALL COTTAGE DISMANTLED

Beyond the open door, a two-wheel cart loaded with household goods and with a cow tied behind it. An old man with a long white beard carrying an inverted glass globe containing artificial flowers, and two chickens. A gaunt, harried woman with a squealing pig under one arm and a churn under the other. Three girls from eigh-

teen to ten rushing in and out with other objects and loading them
into the cart.

> WOMAN
>
> Hurry! Hurry! Do you want everything we own to be
> blown up by those damned Germans? Isn't losing the
> house enough?—without losing everything else, too?

> OLD MAN
> (in a quavering voice)
> We have an army in front of us to protect us. There's even
> to be an attack.

> WOMAN
>
> Attack! Attack! You have lived here two years and you
> have never seen an attack turn around and go backward.
> Hurry! Hurry!

CUT TO:

162 A HEN HOUSE

Uproar of chickens which are slapping and flying wildly about as
Bouffiou and another soldier try to catch them. Enter an Irish-
woman with a broom who begins to beat them. They turn in surprise and duck out. Bouffiou carrying a chicken and the woman
still striking at them with the broom.

> WOMAN
> Thieves! Villains! Robbers!

They escape the broom. Bouffiou turns and waves his hand. The
woman stops striking at them.

> BOUFFIOU
> Come, come, Madam! What does this mean?

> WOMAN
> My hen! You put it back.

She starts forward and raises the broom. The soldiers retreat.

> BOUFFIOU
> What! Insult the uniform with blows of a menial broom.

> WOMAN
> My hen!

BOUFFIOU

Now, now! Do not complain to me about this matter. Make your complaint to Captain Morache. What is one little hen. Wouldn't you sacrifice one hen to save France? To comfort men who tomorrow will gallantly attack your country's invaders.

WOMAN

Attack! Attack! I will show you what an attack is. I will save France.

She begins to beat them with the broom again and they turn and run.

CUT TO:

163 POST OF COMMAND INT AFTERNOON

Office; the colonel, Morache, Delaage, and two other officers at the table with maps.

COLONEL

There will be a heavy bombardment. The attack will be on the twenty-third—five days from now. The Forty-ninth Division will attack in column of brigades. The Ninety-fourth will be brigade on the left. The shock-head of that brigade will be the Second Battalion. Your company will lead. You will send out patrols every night, Morache. We must have information. You understand?

MORACHE

Yes, sir. On the twenty-third.

COLONEL

Zero will be 6:40 A.M. Your objective will be Giancourt. That clear?

MORACHE

Yes, sir.

COLONEL

Good.
> (he rises)

I will see you tonight before you go in.

All salute him. He goes out. Morache sits at the table. Delaage lounges against the wall smoking. The other two officers go out.

MORACHE

So this is it?

DELAAGE

Seems so, doesn't it? I shall learn still more about war this time, I dare say.

Morache is thoughtful, detached. His tone is gentler than it has ever been with Delaage.

MORACHE

Yes.

(he looks at Delaage)

You are the junior officer now, but probably after this starts, nothing will be juniors or seniors or anything much. So probably you and I have about the same chance.

Delaage watches him curiously. Morache looks down at the paper on his desk.

MORACHE

I don't usually do this. I never have before, that is. I—

DELAAGE

Think it might be bad luck?

MORACHE

No—not that. Maybe it's because I've never had reason to do it before—but this time, I—

He takes a cigarette case from his pocket, opens it but does not take out a cigarette. Delaage still watches him, quite coolly.

DELAAGE

I think I get you. You make your parcel up and I make mine. The one who gets back sends the other parcel to the other's people.

MORACHE

Yes—that's it.

DELAAGE

Right. What's your family's address?

MORACHE

Not family—I have no family but my father. He's all
right. It's—

He is intent on the cigarette case. Delaage still watches him.

DELAAGE

I see. You want it to go to Miss Achard.

MORACHE

Yes.

DELAAGE

Right. I will.

MORACHE

Thanks. I'll do the same for you.

CUT TO:

164 DELAAGE'S FACE

It has a curious, sardonic expression on it as he looks down at
Morache.

DELAAGE

To Miss—

He catches himself. Almost laughs and catches himself. Morache
has not looked up—has not noticed him. Now Delaage's expression changes. It is no longer sardonic. We see Morache remove the
cigarettes from the case and stuff them into his pocket—remove
from about his neck a rosary (this will be inside his clothes) and
take a ring from his finger, and put rosary and cigarette case into
a drawer of the desk.

MORACHE

Yes, Just write out your address and I will do it.

He looks up at Delaage now.

MORACHE

You have not known me very long, but long enough to
think I'm pretty hard.
(Delaage says nothing, watching him)
Too hard to ever fall in love?

DELAAGE

(shrugs)

I don't suppose anybody knows anymore where love will strike than where lightning will strike.

MORACHE

No.

He does not look at Delaage while he talks. His tone is quite quiet.

MORACHE

When I found her, I had just come out of the lines. We had had a bad time. That was at Combles and I was pretty well done in. She had been in Paris working and she had come back trying to find her people. We never found them. I don't know what became of them. The village is gone and they have just vanished. She was kind to me—good to me. It was because I was a soldier, I know that—though I believe that she has come to care for me by now. I take that back. I know she has. But it won't last. I know that too. She is young and I'm thirty-five years old. I'm an old man to her. But she has been faithful to me. I know that. But some day she will—

He is not looking at Delaage who is watching him.

DELAAGE

And then what?

MORACHE

(shrugs)

I will wait till that day comes. It has not come yet, and maybe before it does, you will have had the opportunity to deliver this parcel. Then it won't matter.

(he looks at Delaage)

So you will do that?

DELAAGE

Yes.

MORACHE

Good. And I'll do the same for you.

Now his voice and air become official. He takes papers from the desk.

MORACHE

There will be a runner from Brigade before dark. He will

have an evacuation order for Private Marain. You are still officer of the day. You will see that the order is executed at once and that Private Marain is given transport back to the depot. I've got to go to the Colonel.

Morache goes out. Delaage looks after him. Then he comes to the desk and takes the rosary, ring, and cigarette case from the drawer. He opens the cigarette case.

CUT TO:

INSCRIPTION IN CIGARETTE CASE:

Monique and Paul.
We were not. We are.
Third April, 1915.

165   Delaage's face is quite thoughtful. He puts the objects back in the drawer and closes it and sits quite still.

CUT TO:

166   STREET CORNER   NIGHT
The same café. A cart halted before it. A man on the cart talking to the patron on the sidewalk.

MAN
I'm going. I won't stay. An attack. Yes. I've seen them. You take your choice. If you lose—you're robbed and pillaged by the enemy. If you win, by France.

Monique passes, walking fast. We see her face an instant. It is distracted. She hurries on.

CUT TO:

167   POST OF COMMAND   NIGHT   ORDERLY ROOM
A hen roasting on a spit. CAMERA MOVES BACK to pick up Bouffiou, Regnier, and the woman. The woman is pointing at Bouffiou.

WOMAN
He stole it—he—he—he!

REGNIER
Did you steal that hen, Bouffiou?

BOUFFIOU

I—steal—look you!

He points to Regnier's chevron.

BOUFFIOU

You see that? That little stripe gives you lots of liberties.
But when does it authorize you to call a French soldier a
thief?

REGNIER

Attention!
(to woman)
You will be paid for the hen.
You will only have to make your claim to the captain.

WOMAN

Captain! Captain! When you are going to attack tonight?
When none of you may return?

REGNIER

You wouldn't give one hen to beat the Boche, then?

BOUFFIOU

Just what I told her myself.

REGNIER

Attention!
(to woman)
Get on now. The captain will pay you.

WOMAN

Thieves. Pillagers. Ravishers of France!

Regnier pushes her toward the door. We still hear her voice after
she is out of sight.

WOMAN

Thieves! Villains! Robbers!

Bouffiou turns toward the spitted hen.

BOUFFIOU

Now friends, let us eat in God's peace.

He pauses. Turns. A sound of feet. They all watch as Monique
enters, looks hurriedly about and goes on toward the door to the

office and exits. Bouffiou kisses his fingers airily after her, and turns to the spit.

> BOUFFIOU
> Come, brave comrades! Let us eat.

CUT TO:

168 CAPTAIN'S OFFICE NIGHT
Monique enters. Pauses. Looks about. Crosses the room to the door to the captain's quarters. Pauses. Knocks at the door. Then opens it.

CUT TO:

169 CAPTAIN'S QUARTERS
Monique in the door. Delaage turning looking at her. Monique runs toward him.

> MONIQUE
> God forgive me, I had hoped you would be here. You see, I have even come to where I lie to myself. But it's no use, I can't help it. I know now that I have never stopped lying.

She puts her arms about Delaage's neck. He holds her, but stiffly and coldly. She clings to him not noticing that he is cold.

> MONIQUE
> And you go up tonight. And you attack in five days.

> DELAAGE
> How did you learn that? Who has been talking about that?

> MONIQUE
> Everyone in the village knows it. Everyone. Perhaps some woman in love learned it just as I learned it. Five days. Five days. That's exactly half as long as I have known you.

She is trying to kiss him, realizes that he is holding back. She draws back and looks at him.

> MONIQUE
> Pierre, what is it?

Delaage takes her arms away from his neck.

MONIQUE

Pierre, Pierre!

DELAAGE

No.

MONIQUE

No?

DELAAGE

No, not any more.

MONIQUE

You mean you don't love me?

DELAAGE

All right. Call it that.

MONIQUE

Look at me. Will you look at me and say that?

Delaage does not answer. They look at one another.

> MONIQUE
>
> Will you kiss me and still say that?

> DELAAGE
>
> No.

> MONIQUE
>
> No what?

> DELAAGE
>
> I won't kiss you.

Monique approaches and puts her arms about Delaage again.

> MONIQUE
>
> Yes, you will. Only if just goodbye.

Delaage fights against it. They kiss. He takes her arms again and almost flings her away.

> DELAAGE
>
> No. He told me all about it. He gave me the things to give you if he doesn't come back. I didn't know until then. I thought it was just him and me and a girl—a woman. But I know better now. I didn't like him at first. Maybe I still don't. I don't know. But I know what he is doing. Has done with this company. I know what you mean to him. What you have done to him. Let some one else break it up—it won't be me.

Monique stands with her head lowered, motionless. She looks up.

> MONIQUE
>
> Yes—you are right. I told him at first I didn't love him— that it was because he needed me—someone—maybe anyone. But I happened to be there, and that maybe someday I would find—I would find—and he said he would take that chance. Yes, you're right. Let someone else break it up. It won't be I, either. So, goodbye, soldier.

They look at one another. Monique salutes. Delaage turns and goes out. Monique looks at the door.

Then she begins to cry. She lies across the bed crying.

> CUT TO:

170 BIG ROCK A STABLE NIGHT
Replacements are lined up with their packs open at their feet.
They are not at attention. They are quiet. We see that their equipment is in sharp contrast to that of the veterans. Morache and Regnier are moving down the line examining the packs. Morache is
standing. Regnier is stooping over an open pack.

CUT TO:

171 PACK
His ammunition, trench tool, his spade, shovel, gas mask, a big
tin box. We focus on this box.

REGNIER
     Open it!
The soldier's hand opens the box. It contains a miscellany of objects all quite neatly arranged.

REGNIER
     Empty it—dump it out!
The hand empties the box. A small Bible, a jar of home-made jams,
a few bars of chocolate, another object not yet unfolded.

REGNIER
     Throw it away.

SOLDIER'S VOICE
     Throw what away?

REGNIER
     The box. Go on.
The hands throw the box. We hear it strike the floor. It is a tin box.

REGNIER
     Now—that!

SOLDIER
     Now what?
The hand touches the jam.

SOLDIER
     It's good to eat.

REGNIER
    All right—eat it now. The chocolate too.

                    SOLDIER
Now?

                    REGNIER
Yes—now! Now that!

                    SOLDIER
What?
The hand moves on and touches the Bible.

                    REGNIER
Yes—that. Only good to make pipe lighters. You won't
need them until you come out. Go on—throw it.
The hand vanishes with the Bible.

                    REGNIER
What's that?
The hand comes back—opens the last parcel. It is a complete
home-made 'housewife'. Thread, needles, scissors, buttons, etc.

                    REGNIER
Throw it away!

                    SOLDIER
My mother made it for me.

                    REGNIER
That's fine. Throw it away.
The hand vanishes with the 'housewife'.

                    REGNIER
Now make up your pack. Next!!

CAMERA BEGINS TO MOVE BACK. We hear the sound of feet
entering. We now see Delaage just entering as Morache turns to
him. Delaage does not salute.

                    DELAAGE
The company is ready to move.

                    MORACHE
Has the runner come from Brigade yet?

                    DELAAGE
No—not yet.

MORACHE
That's all you're waiting for?

DELAAGE
Yes. All. I have attended to everything else.

MORACHE
Everyone else is cleaned up?

DELAAGE
Yes. Everything. We are just like we were when we came
out. We are ready to move.

MORACHE
Right. Go to your platoon.

Delaage goes out.

REGNIER
Next pack!

CUT TO:

172 ORDERLY ROOM NIGHT
The fireplace—fire still burning. The spit is empty. A few chicken
bones on the hearth and in the ashes.

BOUFFIOU
So you have soldiered before?

OLD MAN
Yes. But no more—it seems. Apparently France does not
need me.

The CAMERA IS MOVING BACK. It picks up Bouffiou's crossed
feet on the desk, as it continues to move—

BOUFFIOU
You are lucky. Why fight? Why suffer and die in the mud?
The prey of ten thousand bullets every twenty-four
hours?

We now see Bouffiou at the table as before. The old man sits in the
chair beside him. He is sad and dejected, leaning forward. His
hands between his knees.

OLD MAN

You have been under fire? You have risked your life for
France?

BOUFFIOU

As you see me. Am I not a member of the Fifth Company? The company of the redoubtable Morache?

OLD MAN

But you are just an orderly. I didn't know that orderlies
fought.

BOUFFIOU

Hah! Ask anyone. Ask Regnier—no—do not ask Regnier.
Do not ask any of them. They do not like me. They will
tell you lies. I'll tell you who to ask.

   (he looks at the old man who has not moved)
You go back tonight?

OLD MAN

Yes. When the order comes.

BOUFFIOU

Then you ask Morache if I do not fight.

OLD MAN

But I probably won't see him.

BOUFFIOU

That is true. He will be busy. Then you will have to take my word for it, won't you?

OLD MAN

Yes.

BOUFFIOU

Then you do take my word?

OLD MAN

Yes. But that I should be refused—who had been passed as fit for service—who once blew the finest calvary in the world—

Footsteps. The old man rouses. A runner comes in with a mail pouch. He slaps it on the table. The old man looks at it with a sad, despairing expression.

BOUFFIOU

How goes it, old son?

RUNNER

Ask yourself that five days from now.

BOUFFIOU

It won't be the first attack I have been through.

RUNNER

Sure. Only some day your beard is going to get tangled up in your puttees and you won't be able to get from that table at all.

The runner takes out the dispatch card.

RUNNER

Where's the officer?

BOUFFIOU

I'll sign it.

RUNNER

Since when. Have you learned to write? You must have been on leave.

BOUFFIOU

Give me the card.

The runner puts the card on the desk. Bouffiou takes out his spectacle case—is about to go through the entire spectacle business again.

RUNNER

Come on! Come on! Put an X on it—I've got to get back.

Bouffiou takes up the pen. The runner guides his hand to the line.

RUNNER

Go on—write something on it.

Bouffiou writes slowly. His mouth working as he writes. The runner takes up the card and looks at it.

RUNNER

Be careful during this next ten days. You may forget how to read too.

The runner goes out. The old man looks at the pouch sadly.

OLD MAN

So it will be in there.

BOUFFIOU

You can't tell. Those guys of Brigade may do anything. They may have even posted you to the Flying Corps, but we'll see.

He empties the pouch on the desk. The old man leans forward. He is both eager and sad.

BOUFFIOU

Let us see.

He goes through the pantomime of the spectacles—puts them on—ruffles through the papers. The old man watching him. He chooses one and opens it.

> BOUFFIOU
>
> Yes—this is it.
> (he turns to the old man, dramatically)
> Monsieur—you are saved.

> OLD MAN
>
> Yes—a little piece of paper. That's all. A little scrap of paper that any flame—even a candle—even a match—

CUT TO:

173 CAPTAIN'S QUARTERS NIGHT
Monique lying face down on the bed.

CUT TO:

174 ANOTHER BILLET NIGHT
The men are lined up. Delaage and a corporal facing them.

> CORPORAL
>
> Trenching tools—

The men throw their trenching tools onto the floor at their feet.

> CORPORAL
>
> Iron rations.

The men throw their iron rations on the floor before them at their feet.

> CORPORAL
>
> Gas masks.

CUT TO:

175 STABLE BILLET
Morache and Regnier are at the end of the line. CAMERA DESCENDS toward the pack at the last man's feet.

CUT TO:

176 PHOTOGRAPH OF FAMILY GROUP
in frame.

> REGNIER
>
> Throw it away.

CUT TO:

177 ORDERLY ROOM NIGHT

The fireplace. The evacuation order on the floor near the fire. As the CAMERA BEGINS TO MOVE BACK—

> BOUFFIOU
>
> This wine must be paid for. Even captains must pay for wine.

We see Bouffiou and the old man facing one another across the desk.

> OLD MAN
>
> All right. How much?

> BOUFFIOU
>
> Do you consider five francs exorbitant?

> OLD MAN
>
> No.

He takes out money.

> BOUFFIOU
>
> I do. But what would you. This is war. In wartime a man is at the mercy not only of all officers and NCOs but of all civilians. Do not forget that.

> OLD MAN
>
> No.

He puts the money on the table. His voice is hushed, repressed and eager.

> OLD MAN
>
> All right. Now. Suppose then—

> BOUFFIOU
>
> Wait!

Bouffiou drinks from the bottle and puts it down.

> BOUFFIOU
>
> Now. Suppose—suppose that little piece of paper was gone—vanished—

> OLD MAN
>
> Then I would go to the front.

BOUFFIOU

Good. Now how could it vanish?

The old man looks at it eagerly.

OLD MAN

How?

BOUFFIOU

Wait.

He takes up the bottle, measures the remaining wine.

BOUFFIOU

Half gone—soon it will be all gone—and then—

The old man takes out more money. He doesn't even count it.

OLD MAN

Here—you can buy more. You can buy a lot.

Bouffiou looks at the handful of money.

BOUFFIOU

True—with all of that. But that is yours.

OLD MAN

No—yours. Take it.

BOUFFIOU

Hah! You're trying to bribe me?

OLD MAN

No—no. I just want to serve France. I just want—

BOUFFIOU

You would die for France if necessary.

OLD MAN

Yes.

BOUFFIOU

Then you surely do not call this a bribe, do you? What can you be thinking of?

OLD MAN

I don't call it a bribe.

BOUFFIOU

You swear? Come—this is a serious business—think!

OLD MAN

I swear.

BOUFFIOU

Good. Give it to me.

He takes the money and puts it into his pocket. He raises the bottle and drinks again. CAMERA BEGINS TO MOVE DOWN toward the paper on the floor. As it moves—

BOUFFIOU

Now just suppose a little wind came—like this—

Sound of gently expelled breath. The paper moves slightly toward the fire.

OLD MAN

(tense and eager)

Yes—yes.

BOUFFIOU

And then a little more wind—like this—

Sound of expelled breath. CAMERA is directly on the paper. It moves again toward the fire. It is still moving at the

CUT:

178 SAME SCENE

The paper is now a charred carbon lying on the hearth. CAMERA BEGINS TO MOVE BACK. We see a pair of feet beside the paper. CAMERA MOVES ON BACK. Regnier is standing over the paper looking down at it. The old man and Bouffiou are very still and quiet. They are alarmed. Regnier turns slowly and looks grimly at Bouffiou.

REGNIER

So that's it! You still say you never saw that evacuation order? Remember, they will have a copy of it at Brigade.

BOUFFIOU

I said I see nothing of it now.

REGNIER

So I heard.

He looks at the old man.

REGNIER

How old are you, actually?

OLD MAN

I am fifty-nine.

REGNIER

So you want to go with us?

OLD MAN

Yes.

REGNIER

I can report you to the captain. He can send you back without the order and have the copy overtake you to-morrow—you know that?

OLD MAN

Yes.

REGNIER

Do you really want to go that bad? This one is not like your war. You won't like it.

OLD MAN

It is still for France. What kind of war—doesn't matter. Whether you like it or not, doesn't matter.

REGNIER

But it may matter to the rest of us. There is one thing in this war that will kill you quick. That's valor and there's another thing that will kill everybody around you. That's cowardice.

OLD MAN

I shall not show cowardice.

REGNIER

You will have to promise more than that.

The old man looks at him. His voice is stubborn, but calm.

OLD MAN

I shall not show cowardice.

Regnier looks at him for a long moment.

REGNIER

Report to your platoon, Private Marain. We begin to move in ten minutes.

CUT TO:

179 SAME SCENE NIGHT

Outside, a voice says, "'Shun—forward march!" We hear rattle of equipment and the tramp of feet on cobbles. Morache enters. Bouffiou stands to attention as Morache passes and goes on into the office. The tramping of feet continues.

CUT TO:

180 CAPTAIN'S OFFICE

Tramping of feet continues. Morache enters. Goes to table. Picks up a paper or two, glances at them—arranges them in order, opens the desk drawer, pauses.

CUT TO:

181 INT DRAWER

He closes the drawer. Goes on to the door to his quarters. The tramping of feet dies away.

CUT TO:

182 MORACHE'S QUARTERS

Monique lying on the bed face down. Morache enters, pauses, sees her. Outside a voice says "'Shun—forward march"—clash of gear, feet begin to tramp past. Morache comes to the bed and puts his hand on Monique's shoulder. She turns, sits up. Her face shows she has been crying.

MORACHE

Crying! This soon? We are not gone yet. I'm not, that is. I shan't go up until midnight.

MONIQUE

Not till midnight—yes.

MORACHE

Aren't you glad of that?

MONIQUE

Yes—yes, I'm glad.

Morache looks at her tenderly. The tramping of feet passes and dies away. Monique rises. He takes her in his arms. She clings to him suddenly.

MONIQUE

Yes, yes—I love you, I love you. I'll try—I'll try.

Morache holds her away so he can see her face. She is crying again.

MORACHE

Try?

MONIQUE

No—no. I do. I do!

MORACHE

Now—now, we have until ten o'clock.

Monique is crying uncontrollably. Morache holds her. His face is suddenly grave.

MORACHE

You're tired—had you rather go home?

Monique clutches him again.

MONIQUE

No—I'll stay. I want to—I do want to. I swear I do.

Voice outside. "'Shun—forward march." Clash of gear. Tramp of feet begins to pass.

MORACHE

You go home. I'll be back in eleven days.

MONIQUE

I'll stay with you until ten. I'll do anything you ask. I swear I will.

MORACHE

I know—come on now.

He puts her cloak over her shoulders and leads her toward the door.

MORACHE

I'll be back in eleven days.

MONIQUE

Yes, eleven days.

She turns suddenly. Clings to him. Still crying.

MORACHE

Now, now—the orderlies are out there. Buck up now.

MONIQUE

Yes—goodbye—goodbye.

MORACHE

In eleven days.

MONIQUE

In eleven days.

She goes out. Morache looks after her. The tramping of feet outside dies away. He turns back into the room. His face is very thoughtful. He crosses the room slowly. He pauses. Stops. The CAMERA BEGINS TO MOVE DOWN to what he is looking at.

CUT TO:

183 DELAAGE'S PENCIL LYING ON FLOOR

Voice outside. "'Shun—forward march." Clash of gear. Tramping of feet again. Passing along.

FADE OUT:

FADE IN:

184 A FRONT-LINE TRENCH NIGHT

Moderate gunfire. Morache and the relieved captain.

MORACHE

So you took care of the mine for me.

RELIEVED CAPTAIN

Yes. Three dugouts went. I lost eighteen men, but I shan't have to take care of your attack for you.

MORACHE

No. This time we won't leave each other rubbish to clean up. At least I hope not.

RELIEVED CAPTAIN

Yes. If there is any rubbish left after this time, it will take more than one company to clean it up.

He looks at his watch.

RELIEVED CAPTAIN

I have only ten minutes to get past the Corner in. As soon as our bombardment starts, they will begin to shell our back areas again.

MORACHE

You had better run.

RELIEVED CAPTAIN

Yes. Good luck to you.

MORACHE

Thanks.

The relieved captain and his orderly go on down the trench. Morache looks at his watch.

CUT TO:

185 THE WATCH

The hands are at twenty-five minutes to two.

186 DOUBLE EXPOSURE WATCH

Hands at fifteen minutes to two. The gunfire increases. It becomes quite heavy.

CUT TO:

187 TRENCH

NCO is hurrying along it. Passes Morache. He lifts the curtain to dugout door.

NCO

Stand to. Stand to. Stand to.

He drops the curtain and hurries on. Men come out of the dugouts. The trench is full of men. The gunfire is quite heavy. Morache looks through periscope. Delaage comes in.

DELAAGE

Our back areas are catching it. Even a bug couldn't get out now.

MORACHE

Yes. You'll lose more than a section this time.

DELAAGE

Quite. But this time I didn't. This time I have a hero to report.

MORACHE

You?

DELAAGE

It was my last section. I saw it myself. It was a shell—a dud. I don't know where it came from. It just appeared out of nowhere, bouncing and rolling right into the middle of the section while they were waiting for the signal to run. One of the replacements threw himself onto it and covered it. Of course it was too late then and it wouldn't have done any good anyway, but he didn't know that.

MORACHE

A replacement?

DELAAGE

Yes. An old man named Marain. How he ever got here in the first place I don't—

Morache turns from the periscope.

MORACHE

Marain?

DELAAGE

Yes. Marain.

CUT TO:

188 CAPTAIN'S DUGOUT

The firing is heavy, but faint and muffled. Morache is sitting at his desk. Regnier and the old man are facing him. Delaage and another officer are in the background.

MORACHE

(to Regnier)

You say the order came but you didn't see it? Why didn't you see it?

REGNIER

It was burned, sir.

MORACHE

Burned?

REGNIER

I saw the ash of it.

MORACHE

Who burned it?
Regnier doesn't answer.

OLD MAN

I burned it.
Morache does not look at the old man. He looks at Regnier.

MORACHE

Who burned it, Regnier?
Regnier does not answer.

MORACHE

So it was Bouffiou.

OLD MAN

No. I did it. The blame is mine.

Morache does not look at him.

MORACHE

(to Regnier)

As soon as the shelling stops you will send Private Marain to the rear with a runner. I will have the order ready.
In the meantime you will be responsible for him. If necessary, you will put him under arrest.

REGNIER

Very good, sir.
(to the old man)
About face—march!

They go out.

MORACHE

Delaage.

Delaage comes forward.

MORACHE

I told you to stay in the office until that runner came. You
were not there.

DELAAGE

Yes. I wasn't there.

MORACHE

Have you any explanation to offer?

DELAAGE

No.

MORACHE

This is your second time in the lines. You should know
something about it now. You should realize that he is a
danger, not to himself, but to the others.

DELAAGE

Yes—I know that.

MORACHE

And now I can't send him out until the shelling stops.

DELAAGE

Why not? He says he wants to die for France. Let him die
at the Corner.

MORACHE

That's good advice. Or didn't Regnier tell you?

DELAAGE

Tell me what?

MORACHE

He is my father.

DELAAGE

What? Your father?

MORACHE

Yes. Good advice, but I don't think I shall take it. I shall
wait until the shelling stops, and I can send a runner
back with him. In the meantime you will remove his
name from your platoon.

DELAAGE

Right. That all?

MORACHE

Yes. That's all.

Delaage turns and goes out.

CUT TO:

189 TRENCH

The gunfire is heavy. Regnier and the old man emerge from the
dugout.

REGNIER

Unless this shelling stops you're going to see your war
after all.

OLD MAN

You helped me once.

REGNIER

Yes. But you had not started jumping on shells then. What was it I told you yesterday? The two things a soldier is not supposed to show because one is about as bad as the other.

OLD MAN

Valor and cowardice.

REGNIER

That's right. And yet you must jump on live shells.

OLD MAN

I said I would not show cowardice.

REGNIER

Maybe better that than being too brave. Get your gear together so you will be ready when the runner goes.

Regnier holds up curtain to dugout entrance. The old man enters. Regnier lets the curtain fall. The gunfire is very heavy. The men crouch along the trench, tense and waiting.

CUT TO:

190 DUGOUT FOURTH PLATOON
The sound of gunfire is faint.

191 CLOSE SHOT AN EARTH WALL
Two deep, vertical scratches are on it, crossed out by a lateral scratch. CAMERA BEGINS TO MOVE BACK.

A VOICE

It's days now, not hours. We have no mine under us now.

SECOND VOICE

But I'd rather see it in hours. It looks like more.

FIRST VOICE

Yes. More of them to wait through until we go out again. What had you rather do—look at two marks crossed out and eight more to go, or at fifty little marks crossed out and four hundred more to go?

THIRD VOICE

Let it be eight to go. Who cares how many are crossed out? It's how many are left that matter.

192   FULL SHOT   DUGOUT

Men playing dominoes, writing letters. Others come down the dugout steps, put their rifles down. CAMERA PANS to the old man on his bunk. Three soldiers are listening to him.

OLD MAN

Fear is only in your mind. There is no such thing as fear. You just imagine it. Say there is a shell coming toward you. You hear it—you hear it come closer and closer—it is going to strike you—but it is not. You do not hear the one that strikes you. You just imagine this fear. It does not even exist—

The men laugh. The laughter drowns out his voice.

FIRST SOLDIER

Did you ever hear a shell coming at you?

OLD MAN

Yes. I was just fourteen, but I blew a charge that the Fifteenth Hussars—

FIRST SOLDIER

But I mean did you ever hear a shell?

The old man looks about at them, trying to speak.

SECOND SOLDIER

He saw one, anyway. He tried to play hobby-horse with it.

OLD MAN

I tell you I—

CUT TO:

193   OUTSIDE THE FRENCH WIRE   NIGHT

Steady gunfire. Regnier and four other soldiers crawl out. The old man is in the center. A flare lights their faces up.

REGNIER

Down—down—down.

The soldiers crouch. The old man's face is still raised, a wild expression on it. A burst of machine-gun fire. The bullets strike the wire behind them. The flare dies.

> REGNIER
>
> All right—come on.

The party moves on. They carry a roll of wire and tools. We see the old man, looking this way and that. He is nervous. He pauses.

CUT TO:

194 A DEAD MAN IN THE WIRE

He is upright, his arm drawn back as though about to throw a grenade.

CUT TO:

195 THE OLD MAN

He takes a grenade from his pocket, is about to pull the pin when Regnier catches him.

> REGNIER
>
> Stop! Stop!

The old man struggles.

> OLD MAN
>
> There! Yonder!

> REGNIER
>
> German, hell! He's not even French any more. He's dead.

> OLD MAN
>
> Dead? Dead?

Regnier looks about. A flare lights his face.

> REGNIER
>
> Down! Down!

He thrusts the old man down. The other soldiers all lie prone. The old man's face is still raised. It has a wild expression on it. Another burst of machine-gun fire rings and sparks on the wire. The old man watches it.

CUT TO:

196 THE DEAD MAN ON THE WIRE

His body moving and jerking as the bullets strike it.

CUT TO:

196A THE OLD MAN

He ducks his head, clutching it in his arms. The bullets cease. The flare dies away. Regnier raises his head and beckons. A soldier crawls up.

> REGNIER
>
> You'll have to take him back.

> OLD MAN
>
> No, no—I'm all right—I can stand it. I will stand it.

> REGNIER
>
> Remember what I told you—not courage, not cowardice.

> OLD MAN
>
> I have not turned coward.

> REGNIER
>
> Don't show either. Do as I tell you, do you understand?

> OLD MAN
>
> Yes, I'm all right. It's not fear. There's no such thing as fear. It's just in the mind.

> REGNIER
>
> Good. Keep it there. Don't use your mind out here. What thinking is necessary out here, I'll do myself. That's what I'm here for, do you understand?

Another burst of bullets rings on the wire. The dead man jerks and flops as the bullets strike him.

> OLD MAN
>
> Yes; I understand.

> REGNIER
>
> Good. Come on then.

They crawl on.

CUT TO:

197 A GAP IN THE WIRE WHERE A SHELL HAS STRUCK IT.

The men are repairing it. They duck again. Another burst of machine-gun bullets.

> REGNIER

Down, down.

The soldier beside the old man is killed. The old man looks at the dead man horrified. Regnier rises and begins to work on the wire again.

> REGNIER

Come on—come on!

The old man starts up—jerks his hand back from the wire and looks at it. He has cut himself. He looks at the blood.

> OLD MAN

Blood! Blood! But it's live blood.

He looks at the dead soldier.

> OLD MAN

He never even saw an enemy. Shot in the back—yet he wasn't retreating.

> REGNIER

Why there—hurry—hurry!

The old man falls to work again.

> REGNIER

Down—down!

They all duck. The old man holds his head in his arm. Burst of machine-gun bullets rings and sparks in the wire.

CUT TO:

198 TRENCH

Regnier and two others lower the dead man into the trench. Two more soldiers help the old man down. He is dazed.

> OLD MAN

Dead—dead! He never even saw an enemy. The man who fired that bullet never even saw him.

> REGNIER

All right. Into your dugout now.

The old man does not seem to hear him. He is dazed.

> OLD MAN

Dead, dead! It's not fear—there is no such thing as fear. It's just in your mind.

The soldiers help him up. The bombardment is quite heavy.

> REGNIER
>
> Take him into his dugout.

> OLD MAN
>
> No such thing as fear.

CUT TO:

199   AN EARTH WALL
The two vertical scratches scratched out. A third vertical scratch—
a hand with a bayonet in the act of crossing it out.

DISSOLVE TO:

200   HEAVY GUNFIRE
A trench. A line of men carrying sandbags. We see the old man—
a shell burst. The old man flinches and cringes.

> REGNIER'S VOICE
>
> Down—down.

The men drop. Another shell burst. Seven or eight men vanish.

> REGNIER'S VOICE
>
> Up! Go on, go on.

They rise—run on.

CUT TO:

201   A SHELL HOLE
The old man and three or four others plunge into it. A shell burst.
A running man is killed.

CUT TO:

202   OLD MAN'S FACE
It is wild. He tries to get up. Regnier holds him down. A shell
burst. The old man struggles. Regnier still holds him. The man
frees himself and stands up. He is defying the shells.

> OLD MAN
>
> You cannot hit me. You do not exist. You are just fear—
> and fear is only in the mind.

The shriek of a shell begins—increases—passes over and bursts
behind.

OLD MAN

There's no fear—no death.

Shriek of a shell—it increases. The old man holds his attitude of defiance. Then he falls—his head in his arms. The shell passes on and bursts behind. A shower of earth strikes him. The old man lifts his face.

OLD MAN

No fear—no death. I defy you! I am I—I live—I cannot be—

Shriek of a shell. The old man ducks his head. The shell passes over and bursts behind him. Shower of earth strikes him. The old man doesn't move. Another shell comes over and bursts behind.

CUT TO:

203 TRENCH

Regnier and the other soldiers carrying the old man. He is in a stupor. The firing is very heavy. Enter a corporal.

CORPORAL

Is he hurt?

REGNIER

No—take him below. If he tries to get out again, arrest him.

CORPORAL

All right.
(to the soldiers)
Take him below.

They carry the old man into the dugout.

CUT TO:

204 A SHELL HOLE

It has water in it. Delaage and Morache are lying in the shell hole in the water. Shells are bursting all around them. Morache has binoculars to his eyes.

DELAAGE

About that pencil—I was there. You know that, I suppose.

MORACHE

And then what?

DELAAGE

Nothing—that's all. I was there, but no more. Do you
understand that?

MORACHE

Why shouldn't I understand it?

DELAAGE

Why shouldn't you? Will you tell me about her again?

MORACHE

I told you. I found her. I tried to help her. She was good
to me. Some day she won't be, but maybe I will be dead
then and it won't matter. That's all.

A shell bursts. Water splashes over them. Another shell. Morache
peers through the binoculars.

MORACHE

Someday she will meet a young man—somebody like
you. But I will wait until that day comes.

DELAAGE

Yes, I suppose she will. But it won't be me.

Morache peers through the binoculars. A shell bursts.

DELAAGE

(continuing)
Do you hear me?

MORACHE

Yes, I heard you.

DELAAGE

It won't be me.

MORACHE

We must get a patrol out there as soon as this shelling
lets up. It will probably stop tonight.

DELAAGE

Did you hear me?

Morache looks at him.

MORACHE

Did I hear what?

DELAAGE

It won't be me.

MORACHE

Thanks.

He looks into the binoculars again.

MORACHE
(continuing)

We must get a patrol out as soon as we can.

DELAAGE

All right. I'll go. You won't have to send me.

Morache looks at Delaage.

MORACHE

Why shouldn't I send you?

DELAAGE

Why not? That's what I would do in your place.

Morache looks at him.

DELAAGE

I'm sorry. I didn't mean that. Everything is just like it was
when we came out. I swear that.

Morache looks through the binoculars again.

MORACHE

Nobody asked you to swear.

DELAAGE

I know it. That's why I do it. Will you accept the oath?

MORACHE

Why not?

DELAAGE

Yes. Why not?

A shell bursts. Another shell. The water splashes up around them.
Morache peers through the binoculars.

CUT TO:

205 DUGOUT
The domino game is going, the men are writing letters. PAN to the old man in his bunk. Three soldiers sitting and listening to him.

OLD MAN
It was not fear. There is no fear. It is only in the mind.
He looks about at them.

OLD MAN
Listen. There is a crisis in a man's affairs which makes him either craven or a hero. It doesn't matter. Valor and cowardice are the same. Anyone may show either of them. It's like an open manhole in the street. You fall into it, and lo! you are either a coward or a hero when you come out—

FIRST SOLDIER
Maybe smelling like a rose or like—

OLD MAN
Wait! Stop! That's it. I have listened for too long a time to what I think I remember—think I know. When we remember it we call it courage. They give you ribbons for it—green and red ribbons to wear—

FIRST SOLDIER
Or maybe a red ribbon for your lapel. But you have to be a civilian to wear it.

OLD MAN
All right. Call yourself civilian.

CUT TO:

206 TWO SOLDIERS
One of them is taking out the old man's battered bugle.

OLD MAN'S VOICE
There is a kind of courage that you buy as you buy tins of milk. I don't mean that kind. I mean—

The soldier raises the bugle to his lips and blows. It makes a raucous tuneless sound.

                                                              CUT TO:

207 THE OLD MAN
He springs up at the sound.

>   OLD MAN
>   It is not fear. There is something in me that I cannot control—

The old man and the soldier are now scuffling over the bugle. The soldier puts it to his mouth and blows a number in raucous, clumsy sound.

>   OLD MAN
>   No! No! Listen—like this!

He takes the bugle himself now and blows his old-fashioned song.

CAMERA BEGINS TO MOVE BACK:

We see a pair of boots, the legs, hands on hips as the man is obviously watching the old man with a good deal of disgust. The faint sound of gunfire increases. He puts the bugle to his lips again. He is trying to drown out the sound of gunfire by blowing his old calls.

                                                              CUT TO:

208 TRENCH NIGHT
Men climbing over the parapet. A shell burst comes, right on the parapet. A few of the men vanish, the others run on. Still more climb over the parapet, running. More shells burst. Still more men vanish.

                                                              CUT TO:

209 DUGOUT
The gunfire is faint and steady. The old man is crouched in a corner with his arm over his face. With each new shell burst, the old man cringes still more into the corner.

210 CAMERA MOVES BACK
We see the battered bugle neglected and forgotten at his feet. Background of heavy, muffled firing.

CUT TO:

211 ANOTHER PART OF DUGOUT

The earthen wall. Three heavy vertical slashes crossed out. A hand with bayonet in the act of crossing out the fourth slash. The firing is faint though steady. The hand has a watch on the wrist. The hand on the watch is at twenty minutes past two. Double exposure over watch to hands at two minutes to two and instead of holding a bayonet the hand now holds a charred cork stopper. Now we can hear a background of voices.

CAMERA MOVES BACK:

We see the night's patrol preparing to go out. Removing their surplus gear, blackening their faces with the charred cork. We see the old man. He is interested but still dejected.

> FIRST SOLDIER
> I owe you ten francs. I square off for six.

> SECOND SOLDIER
> No, I'd rather you owe me the ten. I'll take a chance on your coming back.

> THIRD SOLDIER
> You're betting him ten francs to six that he'll come back tonight. Is that it?

> SECOND SOLDIER
> Not at all. He is to pay me the six francs tonight and if he comes back he'll owe me the other four.

> FIRST SOLDIER
> No. I won't do it.

The old man listens.

> SECOND SOLDIER
> You will not take a ten to six shot against coming back tonight?

> OLD MAN
> (eagerly)

Yes. I will.

They laugh at him. Enter Regnier. His face is already blackened.

> REGNIER
> All right, men. Let's get going.

> FIRST SOLDIER
> Here! Here is a man that wants to go on your patrol with you.

Regnier looks at the old man.

> REGNIER
> You do, do you?

> OLD MAN
> Yes. It wasn't fear. It was just something in me that I could not—

Regnier looks at the others.

> REGNIER
> You draw your grenade at the fire step. Let's go!

The two guards have returned to the checker game, after having reclaimed the corks that the patrol used to blacken their faces with. The old man goes back and sits on his bunk with his bugle.

> OLD MAN
> I've not shown cowardice.

> FIRST GUARD
> But what you have shown hasn't done you much good here. In this war you're not supposed to show either one.

> OLD MAN
> After this—I'll try not to.

> GUARD
> That's fine. Stick to it.

> OLD MAN
> Yes.

> DISSOLVE TO:

212 DUGOUT WALL

Five vertical scratches, hand with bayonet scratching out the last mark.

CUT TO:

213　HANDS ON WATCH

saying forty minutes past ten. Voices in background. This hand holds a piece of cork on the end of a bayonet. We see it hold the piece of cork into the flame of a candle.

AS CAMERA MOVES BACK WE SEE

five men blackening their faces with a piece of cork.

> FIRST SOLDIER
>
> Your own mother wouldn't know you out there tonight.

> SECOND SOLDIER
>
> I hope my mother will not be out there tonight, but if you're not quiet somebody else's mother will be. Madame Mitrailleuse! But she has no children.

> THIRD SOLDIER
>
> What do you mean, no children! When she has been married to death for two years now.

> FOURTH SOLDIER
>
> You seem pretty certain about it.

> THIRD SOLDIER
>
> Why shouldn't I? I'm being paid to do this and I've done nothing else for two years. The women have all the good jobs.

> SECOND SOLDIER
>
> Except bank robbing. There has never been a good woman bank robber. Why should they be. They don't have to go to the trouble to break into vaults.

> REGNIER
>
> Come on! Come on, men!

DISSOLVE:

CAMERA MOVES UP TO CHECKER GAME

Old man's air is still eager, but it is cunning. He looks at the checker game for a while and says:

OLD MAN

If you would make this move you would beat him. Give him this (points) and this man (points) and this third man. Now you take your man here—

He takes up the burnt cork and makes the jump—

And jump him here—and here—and here—

He steps back from the table. One of the players looks at the board. He starts back.

SOLDIER

Where in hell did the cork go?

CUT TO:

214 CAPTAIN'S QUARTERS

Morache and Delaage. Delaage has his face blackened up and he is ready to go out on patrol.

MORACHE

So you still think I'm sending you where I won't go myself?

DELAAGE

No. I didn't mean that. If I ever said it, I didn't mean it and never thought it.

MORACHE

You take my attack tomorrow and I will take your patrol tonight.

Delaage laughs.

DELAAGE

I know your company would suffer and I'm afraid my patrol would suffer as well. You and Regnier are both trying to force me to admit that you know better how to do it than I do. All I want you to do is wish me luck.

MORACHE

I'll do better than that. I'll wish us both luck. I must know who holds that sector. How well it is manned and whether there is a machine gun in that log.

DELAAGE

I can find that out for you easily enough. All I've got to
do is go out there and belch right loud. I'll find that out.
But you would object to that.

MORACHE

Nobody's going to object to it. Well, good luck.

Delaage does not shake hands.

DELAAGE

Good luck.

Delaage goes out.

CUT TO:

215   OUTSIDE THE FRENCH WIRE   NIGHT

Delaage crawls out followed by six men. Regnier brings up the
rear. A flare begins and dies away. Regnier crawls up beside Delaage. They wait until the flare dies.

DELAAGE

Their front turns just yonder. That trench makes a traverse to the left. We can go right past it and then by post
number four, so suppose we try the barn first. So I have
learned something about night patrolling, Sergeant.

REGNIER

You have learned something about war, sir.

DELAAGE

I wish Captain Morache could hear you say that, but
come on, we have five miles to go and daylight begins at
five now.

They crawl on followed by the other men.

CUT TO:

216   ANOTHER PART OF NO-MAN'S-LAND

A flare dies away. A machine gun sounds overhead. Delaage and
Regnier watch it carefully.

REGNIER

Down! Down!

The flare dies after a while.

> That dark blob over there is German wire. We must be absolutely quiet. There are two things on night patrol that everyone must remember or he won't last very long. You kill not only yourself but every one else with you. One of them is cowardice and the other is courage. Do exactly what I tell you—no more, no less.

The men crawl up. One of them is restrained but excited. They notice him. Delaage has him brought up. He dips his handkerchief in a mud puddle and wipes the man's face. It is Old Marain. The flare dies slowly away.

CUT TO:

217 ANOTHER SHELL HOLE

The party of six plunge into it. Regnier and Delaage are carrying the old man. He is hysterical.

(NOTE: The old man's dialog of his hysteria will be written in later. We are trying now to get over the action.)

Delaage and Regnier both hold him.

> REGNIER
>
> What will you do with him, sir?

> DELAAGE
>
> As you see, he must be taken back in. I will take him in by number four post. You will take the patrol, go out as far as the farm, see if that machine-gun post is there, go on as far as that traverse and see if you can capture one sentry, then fall back on post number four.

> REGNIER
>
> Let me take him back, sir.

> DELAAGE
>
> No, I can do it.

Regnier and the others go on. Delaage is now holding the old man. The old man's dialog indicates his hysteria. He realizes he has made a mistake—that he is asking Delaage to give him one more chance, but they both know that he is not accountable for what he might do. They lie in the shell hole. Another burst of machine-gun fire starts. It is sweeping towards them. The old man is hysterical. He would even go through his former pantomime of defying the whole German artillery, but he knows that he is about to reach the point where he will be a danger to everybody. He lies whimpering and panting. His hand over his head. The machine-gun fire sweeps up and past.

> DELAAGE
> Come! Quick now—think of the other men out here.

They rise and run. The old man stumbling. Delaage supporting him.

CUT TO:

218 SAME SCENE POST NUMBER FOUR
Delaage and the old man plunge into a shell hole. Delaage points out to the old man where the post is. The old man is quite hysterical. He has lost his nerve completely.

> OLD MAN
> Let us run for it! Let us run!

> DELAAGE
> Steady—think of those other men out there—think of Regnier!

> OLD MAN
> (whimpers)
> Yes—I will have to think of him. He was good to me once. If it had not been for Regnier—I would not have got here.

The old man begins to laugh hysterically. Delaage holds him. They struggle. We see four or five shadowy figures approaching, stooped over and hurried. The old man sees them suddenly.

> OLD MAN
> Look! Yonder!

He tries to free his arm. Delaage grasps at it. Misses. The old man takes out a grenade and hurls it. The explosion is near the five approaching figures. A cry of surprise from them. Delaage is still trying to grasp his arm. The old man pulls another grenade. The old man's voice is hysterical, whimpering.

OLD MAN
I'm not afraid! I'm not afraid!
Delaage strikes him over the head with his pistol. A machine gun
starts. Shell burst comes. Delaage picks up the old man, runs back
toward the post, stooping. Firing is quite loud.

CUT TO:

219 TRENCH
Men standing to along it at night. Firing very heavy. NCOs shouting down into the dugout. A note of hysteria in the shouting.

VOICES
Here they come! Here they come! Hurry!
As the men come out with their rifles and crouch below the parapet. Morache in foreground. He is watching through a loophole.
He is very grim. The firing is increasing. We see three men hurry
out of a traverse. One carries a light machine gun. Delaage and
another man support the old man. Delaage does not look around.

FIRST OBSERVER
Yes sir—they were coming over fast. The telephone was
still there but I got the gun out.
Morache now looks at the old man. He looks spent—exhausted—
in a stupor. The firing increases.

MORACHE
You split your patrol, then somebody bombed it. Who
threw that bomb?

DELAAGE
I did.

MORACHE
Who threw that bomb, father? Put that man under arrest.
(to Delaage)
You've been hit?

DELAAGE
Yes. Through the hand. It's nothing.

MORACHE

Report to the dressing station. Take Private Marain with you and turn him over to the APM.

Delaage salutes. Turns. Two soldiers lift the old man gently.

FIRST SOLDIER

Come.

Morache is looking back through the loophole. They lead the old man out.

He stumbles along. He is sad and dejected. They take his arms away from him. The firing increases. We see the men up and down the trenches, excited, yelling. They are firing swiftly. They begin to fall back. Morache is the last to hold his ground. A soldier is struck beside him at a machine gun. Morache grasps the machine gun and begins to fire it. The firing becomes very heavy. Artillery rifles, machine guns.

                                                    CUT TO:

220 SHOT OF MEN
Falling stubbornly back. We see Morache with his machine gun
still firing. Shells burst around him. He and his men retreat stubbornly.

                                                    CUT TO:

221 VARIOUS SHOTS FROM *LES CROIX DE BOIS*
showing the French falling back.

                                                    FADE OUT:

FADE IN:

222 FULL SHOT INT CHURCH
CAMERA IS SHOOTING TOWARD THE ALTAR, where a priest
is serving Mass. In the right background, standing against a pillar,
a soldier is singing "Ave Maria."

223 MEDIUM CLOSE SHOT THE ALTAR
A soldier who is serving as acolyte kneels.

224 MEDIUM SHOT CONGREGATION

CAMERA IS SHOOTING FROM ALTAR. The congregation con-
sists of soldiers and civilians from the village.

225 MEDIUM CLOSE SHOT PRIEST
as he raises the Holy Wafer above his head.

226 MEDIUM SHOT CONGREGATION
The worshipers kneel.

227 MEDIUM LONG SHOT INT CHURCH

CAMERA, SHOOTING FROM REAR OF CONGREGATION.
PANS SLOWLY OVER A BOARD FENCE to the other half of the
church, which is being used as a hospital. Beds are filled with
wounded men whose groans can be heard above the strains of
"Ave Maria."

228 CLOSE SHOT MONIQUE
on her knees. She is dressed in the fatigue uniform of a probation-
ary nurse. She dips a scrubbing brush into a pail of water and
scours the floor. She wields her brush energetically for a few moments, then stops to brush the hair out of her eyes with her wrist.
She sits back and listens to the strains of "Ave Maria" which are
heard on the sound track. She looks about her carefully, then rises
to her feet, wiping her hands on her apron.

CAMERA TRUCKS AND PANS WITH HER as she walks through
the ward with her bucket to the edge of the board fence. She puts
her bucket down and goes around the end of the fence into the
half of the church where the Mass is being served.

229 MEDIUM CLOSE SHOT SOLDIER
as he stands by the pillar and continues with his singing of "Ave
Maria."

230 MEDIUM CLOSE SHOT MONIQUE
She stands against the fence on the other side of the congregation
and raises her eyes.

231 CLOSE SHOT STATUE OF VIRGIN MONIQUE'S ANGLE

232 CLOSE SHOT MONIQUE
She gazes imploringly up at the Virgin and begins to pray hesitantly aloud.

MONIQUE
(softly)
Protect Pierre, Our Lady of the Sorrows. . . . And watch
over Paul, too. . . . They accept everything . . . the rain,
the cold, the hunger . . . the days without sun . . . the
nights without sleep . . . the fear and the pain . . . but
let them live—live—live! Let them believe that they will
live until the very end . . . let them always have that
hope . . . always . . .always.

VOICES OF CONGREGATION
(off)
Amen.

The sound of a commotion on the other side of the fence is heard on the sound track. Monique reacts in alarm and starts immediately to leave.

QUICK DISSOLVE TO:

233 INT HOSPITAL SIDE OF CHURCH MEDIUM SHOT GROUP Nurses, orderlies, medical officers, and several patients who can walk cluster around a mud-spattered dispatch rider who is excitedly reporting to the hospital commandant.

DISPATCH RIDER
There is a terrific attack on. All the first aid posts and casualty clearing stations are overflowing.
Monique is seen struggling into the foreground to listen.

HOSPITAL COMMANDANT
What can we do?

DISPATCH RIDER

All hospitals are to clear their beds of every patient that can be moved. And everybody you can spare is to be rushed up to the casualty clearing stations.

The commandant turns to the group and begins bellowing orders.

COMMANDANT

André, fall in the orderlies and load them in a truck. Soissons, fill another truck with supplies—stretchers, anaesthetics, everything,—de Lorde, start moving out everybody you can.

The medical officers and the orderlies melt away, Monique goes up to the commandant.

MONIQUE

You're taking nurses aren't you, Colonel?

COMMANDANT

(hurriedly)

No, no nurses.

He starts to go away. Monique seizes him by the arm.

MONIQUE

(imploringly)

Please, Colonel. Please let me go.

COMMANDANT

(removing her arm)

Sorry, my dear—no women at the front.

He strides off.

234 CLOSE SHOT MONIQUE

A tremendous uproar is going on around her. Orders, shouts, the groaning of the wounded, blowing of whistles, etc. She is nearly frantic.

QUICK DISSOLVE TO:

235 EXT CHURCH NIGHT MEDIUM SHOT TRUCK

The truck is packed with medical officers and orderlies. The ranking medical officer leans out of the truck and shakes hands with the hospital commandant.

> COMMANDANT

You must hurry. Good luck.

They salute. CAMERA PULLS BACK as truck takes off and roars through the street blowing its siren.

> DISSOLVE TO:

236 BED OF TRUCK NIGHT MEDIUM CLOSE SHOT MONIQUE
She is sitting on the floor with a cap pulled down over her eyes, her knees drawn up in front of her. We cannot see her face. Her hands are in her pocket. Next to her sits an old orderly smoking a pipe. He gazes idly at Monique and then takes it big.

237 CLOSEUP MONIQUE'S KNEES
The overcoat has fallen away from her putteed legs, revealing a short expanse of bare flesh above the tops of the puttees.

238 TWO-SHOT
The orderly leans over and raises the bill of Monique's cap. She looks at him in terror. The orderly whistles. Monique grabs him by the arm and beseechingly puts a finger to her lips. The orderly looks at her sharply, nods, and then points to her exposed knees. Monique hastily covers up the hiatus.

> FADE OUT:

FADE IN:

239 INT FOREST NIGHT
Delaage and the old man run along a path. The thunder of firing is heard on the sound track. An approaching shell hurtles down with its horrible gurgling sound. They throw themselves on their faces. It bursts among the trees, lighting the whole forest and covering the scene with flying dirt and torn horticulture.

> DISSOLVE TO:

240 MEDIUM CLOSE SHOT DRIVER'S SEAT HOSPITAL TRUCK NIGHT
The driver, with the dispatch rider beside him pointing the way, advances the throttle. The truck takes a terrific lurch. The sound of distant shelling is heard on the sound track.

241 BED OF TRUCK NIGHT CLOSE SHOT MONIQUE
undergoing the effects of the lurch. She cowers against the old
orderly at the shell fire. He puts an arm around her.

> ORDERLY
> Steady—you're a soldier now.

Monique sits up, looks around her anxiously, pulls her cap down,
and puts her face on her knees.

> DISSOLVE TO:

242 MEDIUM LONG SHOT INT FOREST NIGHT
Delaage and the old man are seen running along. Another shell
comes. They throw themselves on their faces. The shell bursts.

> DISSOLVE TO:

243 MEDIUM SHOT STRETCH OF ROAD NIGHT

CAMERA SHOOTS DOWN THE ROAD. Shells are falling in its
vicinity. The road is sporadically lit by flares.

244 CLOSE SHOT DRIVER'S SEAT
The sound of the motor is heard on the sound track.

> DRIVER
> (shouting)
> But I can't go down there.

> DISPATCH RIDER
> You've got to. Hurry up!

The driver throws the car in gear and lets in the clutch.

245 MEDIUM LONG SHOT ROAD NIGHT
The car lurches and sways down the road at full speed. Shells fall
about it but do not hit it.

246 BED OF TRUCK NIGHT CLOSE SHOT MONIQUE
She cringes at the detonation of the shells, burying her face in her
hands.

> DISSOLVE TO:

247 ROAD IN FOREST NIGHT
CAMERA PANS with the truck as it dashes down the wooded
road, shells bursting around it.

DISSOLVE TO:

248 ANOTHER ROAD NIGHT MEDIUM CLOSE TRUCKING SHOT DELAAGE AND OLD MAN
plodding along. Delaage is using a stick he picked up in the forest for a cane. The cannonading is less loud on the sound track. Behind them they hear the blowing of a siren. They stop and turn. Delaage raises his stick.

249 MEDIUM SHOT ROAD NIGHT
showing the headlights of a car approaching.

250 MEDIUM SHOT ROAD NIGHT
The car stops by them with a shrieking of brakes. It is an ambulance.

> DELAAGE
> (to driver)
> Two casualties here. Flesh wound and shell shock.

> DRIVER
> You'll have to ride the running board, sir. I'm full up inside.

Delaage and old man mount the running board and hang on to the side of the ambulance. The car drives off.

FADE OUT:

FADE IN:

251 MEDIUM LONG SHOT CHAPEL NIGHT
It is a small edifice. In the foreground in a kind of square there is the great confusion that attends military movements. Motorcycles whizz by, ambulances rush in, a field gun is bogged in the mud, noise and chaos. The sound of heavy firing is heard not far off.
The medical truck juggernauts its way through the confusion and draws up at the steps of the chapel. The men near the end gate jump to the ground.

QUICK DISSOLVE TO:

252 MEDIUM SHOT TAIL OF TRUCK NIGHT
A medical officer stands on the ground talking to a priest. As the men descend, their overcoats billow out. A sergeant stands at the

other side of the end gate bawling at them to fall in, which they
do a few yards from the truck.

> PRIEST
>
> I think, Captain, the best place for your casualty clearing
> station would be right here in our chapel.

> MEDICAL OFFICER
>
> Thank you, Father.

His eyes turn idly to the tail of the truck, from which the men are
jumping. He sees something which makes him start.

253 CLOSEUP MONIQUE'S FEET
Encased in worn slippers, they stand poised hesitantly at the tail
of the truck.

254 MEDIUM SHOT TAIL OF TRUCK
The officer and priest look up at her. CAMERA PULLS BACK to
show Monique jumping. Her overcoat billows out, revealing her
bloomers above her putteed legs. The medical officer seizes her by
the arm and pulls off her cap.

> MEDICAL OFFICER
>
> A girl? What's the meaning of this?

> MONIQUE
>
> Oh, please, Monsieur, let me stay. I'm a nurse. You need
> me. Please let me stay—please.

The priest puts his hand on the medical officer's arm.

> PRIEST
>
> Let her stay, Captain. She's right. We shall need her.

The medical officer releases Monique's arm.

> MEDICAL OFFICER
>
> All right. Take off that absurd coat and report to the ser-
> geant inside.

Monique, ecstatic, dashes out of the shot. The officer shakes his
head at the priest.

> MEDICAL OFFICER
>
> Bad business, Father—a woman up this near.

DISSOLVE TO:

255 FULL SHOT STRETCH OF NO-MAN'S-LAND NIGHT
showing the effects of the heavy bombardment.

FADE OUT:

FADE IN:

256 FULL SHOT INT CHAPEL
A scene of terrific uproar and confusion. Bodies of the wounded are lying everywhere save in the two aisles leading to the altar. Monks lug in cots and set them up against the walls. Stretcher bearers carry newly arrived wounded up the aisles. On the sound track are heard the groans of the wounded and the bawling of orders, and the sounds of distant firing.

257 MEDIUM SHOT CHAPEL DOOR

CRANKING DOWN from inside. A stream of stretcher bearers, walking wounded, and casualties assisted by comrades clogs the entrance, one of the doors of which is shut. A monk hastily unfastens the bolt at the bottom and swings the blocking door back. A maelstrom of damaged humanity gushes through.

258 MEDIUM SHOT ROW OF WOUNDED ON FLOOR
A doctor in the foreground is swiftly cutting the tunic sleeve off a wounded man. Monique comes into the shot. She is in her nurse's uniform and carries a basin of water. CAMERA TRUCKS with her as she hastily goes down the line peering anxiously into the face of each wounded man. Finally she comes to one and stops in terror.

259 CLOSE SHOT CASUALTY ON STRETCHER MONIQUE'S ANGLE
CAMERA PANS SLOWLY UP the body of the casualty, whose arms are folded across him. On his sleeve is the bar of a lieutenant. On his collar device are the numerals "39." A cloth covers his face.

260 MEDIUM CLOSE SHOT MONIQUE
Stifling a scream, she swiftly kneels down beside the dead man and gently draws back the cloth from his face. We do not see the face. Monique puts the cloth back. We know that it is not Delaage.

DOCTOR'S VOICE
(off)
Nurse!

Monique picks up her basin and hastens out of the shot.

CAMERA PANS RAPIDLY to the foot of the altar, where the medical officer we saw at the opening of the sequence and the priest are standing.

MEDICAL OFFICER
Sorry, Father, we'll have to use the altar. There's no more room in here and it's raining outside.

PRIEST
Certainly.

At a signal from the medical officer two stretcher bearers bring in a stretcher with a wounded man on it and deposit it on one of the wide ascending levels leading up to the altar. Monique hurries into shot. The medical officer glances at the man on the stretcher.

MEDICAL OFFICER
(to Monique)
Fetch Captain Jourdain and tell him to bring an ether cone.

He kneels by the stretcher.

261 CLOSE SHOT STRETCHER
The man in the stretcher is one we will recognize from having seen him a number of times previously. On the other side of the stretcher opposite the medical officer is another man we also know. His head is bound with a bloody bandage. He holds the hand of the man in the stretcher. This scene is a paraphrase of the death of Corporal Breval in *Les Croix de Bois*. We will call the man in the stretcher Marou, and the man holding his hand Brouc. Marou fights horribly for breath, and groans as the doctor gently begins unbuttoning his tunic. Tears stream down his face. He is sweating terribly.

BROUC
Listen, Marou—don't give up. It's fine to be wounded. We're going on a long leave together.
(to medical officer)
Aren't we, doc?

MEDICAL OFFICER

That's right. On a good long rest.

MAROU

No—no. . . . I'm done for. . . . I'm not bawling for myself. . . . It's for my little girl—

BROUC

Don't talk so much, pal. You'll wear yourself out.

MAROU

Never mind that. . . . Jean, will you promise to do something for me?

BROUC

Sure, pal—but you'll do it yourself.
          (to medical officer)
Won't he, doc?

MEDICAL OFFICER

          (looking up from work)
Of course.

MAROU

Go to my wife and tell her . . . what she did wasn't
right. . . . Tell her she broke me up . . . bad. . . .

BROUC

Aw, don't talk that way, pal.

MAROU

No . . . no . . . you've got to tell her . . .
          (furiously)
Tell her I put a curse on her before I died . . . and I spit
in the face of her and her guy. . . . Do this for me, Jean—
and tell the whole world what she did when I was at the
front . . . gettin' killed. . . .
          (weeping)
Oh . . . oh . . . no . . . no . . . for the little kid . . . we
mustn't. . . . Just tell her she must be very good . . .
from now on . . . and I'll forgive her. . . .

His body twitches and stiffens, and his head falls back.

BROUC

Remy! Remy!

DISSOLVE TO:

262 ATMOSPHERIC SHOT
Monique's face, agonized by her experience in the hospital, fills the screen. Superimposed are the faces of the wounded and dying, the endless lines of stretchers, the faces of officers bawling orders, the priest uttering prayers of absolution, a surgeon's gloved hand holding a scalpel, etc. On the sound track are heard the booming of the guns, the clang of ambulance bells, the groans of the wounded, and the cries of "Nurse . . . nurse . . . nurse!"

DISSOLVE TO:

263 MEDIUM LONG SHOT SECTION OF DEVASTATED VILLAGE NIGHT
An enemy shell lands on a building, making the walls topple. Several French soldiers rush into the shot in the foreground and disappear around the corner of a building.

DISSOLVE TO:

264 INT VESTMENT ROOM CHAPEL NIGHT CLOSEUP SINK
A basin containing surgical instruments of all kinds stands under a stream of hot water which is coming from a tap.

CAMERA PULLS BACK revealing Monique standing exhausted at the sink. She smooths the hair out of her eyes with the back of a rubber glove and feels the water. The old orderly who sat beside her in the truck comes in.

ORDERLY
Are those instruments sterilized, my dear?

MONIQUE
(wearily)
I think so. I scrubbed them all.

The orderly takes the basin, carefully pours off the water, and is about to start out of the room when he looks at Monique.

ORDERLY
Why don't you rest a moment? They're going to bring the new ones in here. There's no more room in the chapel. Even the altar's filled up.

MONIQUE
(dully)
All right. I will.

The orderly pats her on the shoulder and leaves. Monique slowly peels off her rubber gloves, goes to a chair, and sits down. On the wall behind her hang stoles, chasubles, cowls, and other clerical vestments. Almost immediately her head drops forward and she starts to doze.

265 MEDIUM CLOSE SHOT DOOR OF VESTMENT ROOM
Delaage, his arm around the old man's shoulder, enters with Morache's father. The old man has gone completely to pieces.

OLD MAN
(hysterically)
Those poor fellows in there—all on account of me.

DELAAGE
(gently)
Now, now—

He leads him over to a chair against the wall on the left side of the door. Monique's chair is against the wall on the right.

OLD MAN
If I hadn't thrown that bomb the attack wouldn't have started.

Delaage bends over him and seizes him by the hand.

DELAAGE
(earnestly)
There's no truth in that whatsoever. Please believe me.

OLD MAN
(withdrawing his hand)
How can you touch me? I've disgraced myself . . . my regiment . . . my country . . . my son.

With a groan he buries his face in his hands.

266 CLOSE SHOT MONIQUE
She wearily raises her head, opens her eyes, and sees Delaage.

> MONIQUE
> (almost screaming)
> Pierre!

She springs to her feet.

267 MEDIUM CLOSE SHOT DELAAGE
He whirls around, sees her and rushes forward. CAMERA PULLS
BACK as they dash into each other's arms.

268 TWO-SHOT
They babble swiftly, hysterically, at each other between kisses.

> MONIQUE
> Oh, Pierre, Pierre, my darling . . . my life.

> DELAAGE
> Monique, Monique . . . my love!

> MONIQUE
> I knew I'd find you.

> DELAAGE
> And I thought I'd be dead before I could tell you how I
> adore you.

> MONIQUE
> Oh, my precious!

They embrace.

> DELAAGE
> It was on account of Morache I said I didn't.

> MONIQUE
> I knew.

> DELAAGE
> I couldn't hurt him.

> MONIQUE
> No.

DELAAGE

But I don't care any more. It's all different now.

They embrace again. Suddenly, as though he were conscious that somebody was watching them, Delaage raises his face and looks at the door. Monique looks at him and then in the same direction.

269 MEDIUM CLOSE SHOT DOOR

Morache is standing there staring at them.

270 BIG HEAD CLOSEUPS DELAAGE AND MONIQUE

As they stare off at Morache. Monique tears herself from Delaage's arms.

MONIQUE

I did it! I am the one. He told me weeks ago, that we were through—that there would be nothing else between us—

Delaage steps forward. Pulls her away from Morache.

DELAAGE

I did this. She's lying. I chased after her just like I chased after every woman since you've known me. Just like you always knew that I—

The orderly moves forward leading Morache.

ORDERLY

Give the captain a chair there. Can't you see that he's blind?

Monique falls back as the orderly leads Morache to a chair. Monique runs forward.

MONIQUE

You're hurt! You're hurt!

She starts to cut the sleeve off his arm. Morache puts her aside.

MORACHE

Wait! Who else is here?

DELAAGE

I'm here, Paul.

MORACHE

How are the men?

MONIQUE
Get him a doctor—quick! Quick!

MORACHE
Wait! I'll take my chances with the rest of them.
        (to Delaage)
Are you all right?

DELAAGE
Yes. Just in the hand.

MORACHE
I saw Routhelet and Charpentier killed myself. So you're
in command of the company. Go out and get them together and find out how many men we've got.

DELAAGE
        (pauses)
But about Monique—about—

MORACHE

All right. Go and get the company together—and send
me the adjutant.

Delaage goes out.

MONIQUE

Paul! It was love, Paul—I couldn't help it. But it will happen no more. Do you want me to swear that?

Adjutant enters.

MORACHE

All right. Just a minute now.
(to adjutant)
Well—

ADJUTANT

We have fallen back along the whole front, but the telephone line to post number four is still intact.

MORACHE

Then all we need there is an observer, for five minutes.

ADJUTANT

Yes, sir.

MORACHE

Five minutes will do it.

ADJUTANT

Yes, sir.

Morache rises. Helps himself up by the chair. Monique watches
him.

MORACHE

(to adjutant)
Are you near the door?

ADJUTANT

Yes, sir. Right behind me.

Morache moves toward adjutant. Monique watches him.

MONIQUE

But—Paul—you can't see!

The old man rises.

> OLD MAN

I will be his eyes tonight.

The old man comes forward and takes Morache by the arm. Monique runs forward.

> MONIQUE

No—no—you can't!

> MORACHE
> (to adjutant)

Put this woman under arrest too if necessary, Lenoir.

> ADJUTANT

Very good, sir.

He holds Monique who struggles. He holds her while Morache and the old man go out. Monique struggles awhile and then breaks down. Delaage enters. As Delaage enters he says:

> DELAAGE

Fifty-nine men under arms, sir—where's the captain—where's Morache?

> MONIQUE

He's gone. He's gone to try to find that telephone line. He is gone to die—

Delaage runs out.

CUT TO:

271   A ROAD   DARKNESS

Delaage is struggling against the backward-moving line of troops. He is anxious—hurrying.

CUT TO:

272   ANOTHER PART OF ROAD   DARKNESS

The old man leading Morache. They are struggling against the backward-moving line of troops.

CUT TO:

273   A HILLCREST

Delaage reaches it and looks over. We see the flash of shells begin in the valley. They are becoming quite heavy.

CUT TO:

274 OBSERVATION POST NUMBER FOUR
The old man leads Morache into it. The old man digs up the telephone wire. Morache establishes communication with the rear through it.

> MORACHE
> Now, Father—tell me where the first shell falls.

The old man is nervous and trembling but he is determined to carry on this time.

> MORACHE
> (into telephone)
> Fire!
> (to old man)
> Watch, Father!

A shell burst. The old man is watching.

> OLD MAN
> It was two hundred yards away and to the right, Paul.

> MORACHE
> (into telephone)
> Number two—eight o'clock.
> (to old man)
> Now watch, Father!

The old man watches. Shell burst comes.

> OLD MAN
> That was straight past and fifty yards away, Paul.

> MORACHE
> (into telephone)
> Six o'clock at number one.
> (to old man)
> Now watch, Father!

The old man watches. The shell burst this time seems to be right behind the observation post.

> MORACHE
> Where was that, Father?

OLD MAN

That was close. Can I blow now?

MORACHE

Yes, you can blow now.
(into telephone)
Fire.

The old man takes out his battered bugle. He raises it and begins to blow. The shells burst fast all around the observation post. The gunfire increases.

CUT TO:

275   HILLCREST
Delaage watching the shells falling in the valley. They begin to burst in an orderly line. The line begins to move forward. Shell bursts and firing become very heavy. In the background we hear voices begin to yell—

VOICES

Forward!

CUT TO:

276   A TRENCH
Sound of gunfire. Voices yelling. We see men spring down into the trench, climb out and run out. The leader of them is Delaage.

CUT TO:

277   OBSERVATION POST
Firing is still continuous and men yelling. The observation post is obliterated. We seem to pass it running. We see a section of telephone line and the old man's battered bugle. The men run on. The shelling begins to die away.

FADE OUT:

FADE IN:

278   ON A FRENCH FARM
Soldiers sitting around. They are very weary, cleaning equipment, talking.

CUT TO:

279 DOORWAY
Over the doorway a small sign:

> O.C. Fifth Company
> 39th Regiment

PAN INTO OFFICE

We see Monique in Delaage's arms. This is going to be a love scene. Delaage tells Monique that there is to be a parade in which the company will receive a decoration for Morache and the old man's graves.
An orderly enters.

ORDERLY
The replacements have come, sir.

DELAAGE
All right. In just a minute.

CUT TO:

280 FARMYARD DAYTIME
Replacements lined up. They are very stiff and soldierly. Their equipment in sharp contrast to that of the veterans.

SERGEANT
Come on! Come on! Fall in line there!
The replacements come to sharp attention. Veterans still very careless.

SERGEANT
'Shun!
(turns to face door beneath sign)
Delaage comes out. He makes the same sort of speech that Morache has made twice. Then tells them there will be a parade in ten minutes.

CUT TO:

281 VARIOUS SHOTS OF THE VETERANS
They are grumbling about the parade. NCOs passing among them.

NCOs
Come on! Come on! Snap out of it!

NOTE: The NCOs finally get the veterans into line—get them started—they are marching at ease. They shuffle along with their packs and such, asking one another "What the hell anybody wants to get a decoration for." They begin to move. Presently we begin to hear military music. We see the veterans pull themselves together—begin to straighten up and get into step. The military music grows louder. The veterans have straightened up.

CUT TO:

282   FIFTH COMPANY
Delaage at the head of it. He is marching to attention too. Gradually we begin to see the face of the two men at the head of the company. The old man leading his blind son—they march on. The music is getting louder and louder.

FADE OUT:

END

Afterword

By George Garrett

We know the basic facts of life behind the creation of this film script. From Joseph Blotner's biography, as well as from other scholarly and critical studies, we know now how William Faulkner went out to Hollywood to work on this project. Went to work out of commonplace need and with an uncommon urgency. The need was, of course, for money. Survival money. His books had not sold (and would not sell much for a long long time). His stories weren't finding happy homes. There were not any other easy possibilities, and this was a full generation before serious American writers could find for themselves places in the universities and sell off a portion of their precious time for money. Time was more precious than ever for him at just that time. Never mind the details of his personal, private life. They were complex and aggravating enough. But the true urgency was that he was desperately trying to complete a draft of *Absalom, Absalom!* And, in fact, he managed to finish the complete draft while he was out there working on the property which would become *The Road to Glory.*

All that we need to know, to think about here and now, is that this very great writer under very great pressure, at a time when his life was troubled, when his drinking was a serious problem—enough so that it could easily have cost him the chance even to

159

hold down the assignment on the picture, when time to complete his work-in-progress had to be bought and paid for, earned the hard way by hard labor, parceling out his time and energy and creativity, like a gambler nursing cards and chips over a long night's game for the highest stakes, while holding in reserve within himself the secret, invaluable, still unrecognized treasury of his word-hoard, that this great writer, one of our precious few masters in this century, managed to get the movie job done, also, and to do it well. For even at this stage, a while before the final shooting script, which would come along all in due time, it is a first-class professional job of screenwriting done, as it had to be, in brief, intense collaboration with a whole group of first-class professionals, ruthlessly demanding, utterly unsentimental movie people. More about them, more about all that a bit later.

Here at the outset we need to acknowledge that there were real difficulties which had to be overcome and were, and we need to draw at least some of the inferences which are simply there. For instance, we are obligated to recognize his courage. The risks were then, as now and always, very great. These risks did not, of course, include all of the corruptions of success you can read about in boring and conventional Hollywood novels. His very modest salary, a boon to him but a bargain for his bosses, was not likely to corrupt anybody. What could have happened, what has happened to many talented and evidently stouthearted, strong-willed writers and artists in that brutal milieu, was that he would have been drained of energy, shattered of the confidence needed to take the wild artistic gamble and surmise from which every rare artistic achievement, and also the cemetery of countless artistic failures, these latter, though unlucky, being often every bit as brave, as honest and as well-intended as the fortunate few survivors, derives. To save his real life, which was always a work-in-progress, he had to risk losing it. We can safely infer that William Faulkner was at the time brave enough and tough enough and possessed of faith enough, if not in himself then of his gifts, to do what he had to, whatever he had to at whatever risk. Which means, among many other things, that he was almost perfectly attuned to the spirit of the French combat veterans in this story. One can say, and we will, that in a literary sense he was exactly the right man for this story; but we should also understand that in an inward and spiritual sense he was singularly appropriate to the task. For he understood, at the deepest and most ineffable levels of himself, the inner lives of these characters. And all this comes through quite clearly in the screenplay.

Almost without exception, screenplays, like the finished films they sometimes become, are committee work, characterized by all the familiar confusion, interchange, friction, clash, and compromise that any attempt to create anything by a group consensus inevitably arouses. In the making of screenplays and movies the inherent problems are intensified because of the differences in rank and authority and practical experience among the members of the group. Almost without exception the writer is awarded an unenviably low place in the hierarchy. And yet, paradoxically, it is an essential position, absolutely necessary and important at least until a satisfactory, usable, workable screenplay exists and has been accepted as such by everybody else concerned. This group, the number and variety of people concerned with any given script, ranging from important peripheral types like bankers and lawyers and accountants and agents and casting directors through the entire production company in all its component parts, all the cast and the huge, skilled crew, to the people at the other end who must promote and distribute the finished film, is very large and various. The script must serve all of them and most of them quite differently. It becomes a crucial document in a variety of ways. And it is the writer's responsibility.

Two things need to be said and understood about all this, as it relates to the film. First, we have to understand that there is no way simple and truthful to attribute authorship, in a conventional literary sense, to a screenplay. Everyone concerned contributes one way or another and to a greater or lesser extent. The writer, in essence, becomes for a time the voice or spokesman of the committee and, indeed, the larger group which the committee comes to represent. In the sense of a poem or a short story or even a novel there is no screenplay author at all. (Of course, we should remember that the finished product, the printed book, the actual object itself by means of which we can come to know and experience the words and work of the creator, has engaged the professional services and attentions of a great many people and can, in that strict sense, almost as much as any movie, be said to be the work of a group, an institution, rather than any individual. Writers, after all, write manuscripts. Publishing companies publish and seek to sell books.) Nevertheless, credit for screenplays is in fact earned and given; and this attribution is controlled by a variety of rules. So that no matter how many people in how many ways may or may not have contributed toward the creation of the screenplay for *The Road to Glory*, the official credits are to Joel Sayre and William Faulkner for both the story and the screenplay.

In any collaboration of this kind it is, finally, impossible to distinguish who contributed what since ideas, notions, whims must be blended and fused together into a unity which is largely inextricable, into the sources of the bits and pieces which make up its parts. In other words, another paradox if not an outright contradiction, it doesn't matter, except for the quality of the final film, how many contributions have been made by how many different people, the screenplay is created by the author or authors who are credited with it. Thus the rules of the Guild (the Screenwriters Guild in those days, today the Writers Guild of America, West or East) reflect that reality. And so it follows that we can, honestly and accurately, discuss all aspects of this screenplay as the work of William Faulkner, with the understanding that he shared the authorship equally with Joel Sayre.

What I am trying to suggest is that it would be pointless, and probably wholly inaccurate, to attempt on the basis of external and internal evidence to isolate precisely the separate contributions of either writer to the finished whole or to separate those contributions from the suggestions and even the specific demands (made much more often in discussion than in writing) of the producer and the director, and so forth. Even documents would not, do not, prove much. The crucial single document, at any stage of the development of a picture from idea to film, is the officially accepted version of the screenplay at that stage. Attempts, by those who were actually involved, to disentangle the complex process into its component, individual parts later on are not of much value or authenticity either. Even when (rarely!) recollection is honest and clear, it is neither easy nor accurate to isolate one item or another as originating exclusively from a specific source. All that we have to go on is the composite and finished object, the screenplay. Thus the convenience of credit, of attributed and accepted authorship, turns out to be the only fact of the matter worth worrying about.

With all due respect to Faulkner's collaborator and partner on this film, it is Faulkner's involvement and authorship that matter to us now. Simply for convenience in this afterword, and with full acknowledgment of Joel Sayre's full share in its creation, I intend arbitrarily to talk about this screenplay as Faulkner's. It should be noted, though, that the seamless collaboration evident in this screenplay indicates another truth about Faulkner—an ability to work well and closely and honorably with another writer when he had to. This is certainly not a unique ability, but a great many gifted writers have found that they simply could not collaborate effectively.

The collaborative process of *The Road to Glory* must have been more than usually complicated and demanding. Working for Darryl F. Zanuck was, evidently, an unusually stressful experience; and the evidence is that he fiddled with and fine-tuned several versions of this screenplay between the first surviving version, this version, by Faulkner and Sayre, and the final shooting script. But this film was top-heavy with talent, quite aside from Zanuck. Zanuck's assistant producer was the screenwriter Nunnally Johnson. Who, we can be sure, made himself responsibly influential. And the director, evidently from the beginning, was Howard Hawks. Who would, significantly, continue to use Faulkner on film projects for years to come. Plenty of talent and ego there. It is safe to assume that Faulkner and Sayre had to work with at least three bosses, two of whom legitimately knew more about screenwriting and filmmaking than both of the collaborators taken together. And all three must, unquestionably, have been very powerful and often contradictory presences during the process of creating the script.

A writer, who went to Hollywood in the fifties to write a script for Stanley Kubrick, has told me that he had occasion and opportunity to ask William Faulkner's advice. "Don't take the work too seriously," Faulkner is said to have told him. "But you take these people very, very seriously." As one who has gone down that long row to hoe, myself, I cannot imagine better advice. Or more difficult advice. It is hard not to take the work seriously. That is, all of

the artist's impulses, taken together with his acquired profession-
alism and his earned sense of honor—an essential and ritual sense
of honor which demands complete, unstinting integrity and com-
mitment must be engaged in every exercise of his craft, be it ever
so humble and insignificant; demanding not that it be "good" or
"important," but that whatever it is, it should represent his best,
all that he has to give to that subject and occasion at that moment;
demanding all this at the very grave risk that any conscious lapse
from duty, that any withholding, slacking off, or saving of self and
gifts for some more serious purpose and occasion may result, most
likely *will* result in the permanent loss of a certain kind of purity,
something like artistic virginity; and that loss bearing with it the
even more grave prospect that the Muse will no longer visit the
house defiled not by commerce or greed or strange passions but
by indifference—combine to make him wish to create the best possible screenplay, once he is engaged in and, for one reason and
another, committed to complete the chore.

But that way, the natural way for the artist to work, leads to
crippling frustration and, thus, to poor and shoddy work. It over-
looks the essence of the creative process in movie making—that it
is corporate, that it is political, also, in the sense that the final
product is a choice arrived at through constant negotiation and
compromise. I remember hearing, many times concerning any
number of projects, the old cliché of the business, "If everybody
involved got fifty percent of his ideas into the final version, it
would be the greatest picture ever made." This was almost always
followed by a shrug and a faint smile. "What the hell," they'd say,
smiling and shrugging, "it's only a *movie*." To which should be
added yet another old saw, tossed around like a frisbee in the industry and largely ignored outside of it, to wit, "Nobody ever *tried*
to make a bad picture."

All this was obviously understood by William Faulkner. (Remember that he was speaking to a fellow workman and professional. His comments addressed to others, to outsiders, in inter-
views and such, tended to reach for humor and to satisfy the
preconceptions of outsiders, to tell them more or less what they
wanted to hear, and would hear in any case, about the subject.
Knowing that they would not understand anything else and no
doubt believing that they had no right to try to understand the

artist's choices, his risks and wounds, no right to presume to stand in his shoes.) All this was understood by him and is implied by him in his reply to the younger writer. It is also suggested, if you pause to think about it—and the remark was, like many of his apparently offhand comments, made to make the hearer pause and, perhaps, think about it—that to do good work, to do the work well, which, after all, is the proper aim of every artist and craftsman and is also a matter of simple, commonplace pride and honesty, the desire to earn fairly the money one is being paid for the job, one must be loose, light on his feet, quick, adept, flexible, supple. The work can break your heart if you let it, and that will carry over into all your other work. *Don't take the work too seriously.* If you do, it won't be any good. If you do, you won't be any good. If you do, it will be harmful to you.

As for the people. His advice is well taken also. All of the clichés and stereotypes have roots in the truth. They, the movers and shakers, the wheelers and dealers of the motion picture crap game which they call, partly out of a deep and deeply frustrated desire for respectability, The Industry, are, just as depicted in so many of the plays and novels, and even movies, about Them, rude and crude, gross and sly and greedy and ignorant and ruthless, cruel and funny, and dedicated to . . . *something.* Hard to say precisely what that something is. Yes, they want to make good pictures that make good money and, as a spinoff, offer them a little prestige and repute. Yes, they enjoy dealing and, yes, too, the power to treat with and often to mistreat artists and craftsmen, their envied betters, the power to humble others by constant giving and withholding. (Oh, in a very literal sense, everyone who works in The Industry is reamed on a real or metaphorical casting couch. There are endless stories, many of them true enough, of how They have savaged artists, how they have used them up and discarded them without qualm or even second thought.) So part of Faulkner's advice was, predictably, to stay awake and alert, to watch out. Don't take Them lightly. They can tear you to pieces.

But there is more to it than that. I believe that he understood Them more deeply than that. Understood that these arrogant and insensitive, sly and shifty, slippery and shrewd, wildly piratical codgers, aesthetic gangsters, probably moral cripples, babbling their Immigrant English as they sought to con everyone around them, restrained only and finally, and only slightly, by the Law, They were nevertheless deeply dedicated to a number of things, at least to all of the things, the implausible, manifold combinations of energies, talents and things which are necessary to transform an idea, a whim, a notion into ninety minutes, or more, of finished film to be shown in theaters to people who could be persuaded to pay good money to come inside and see it.

And most of all, beyond even the excitements and challenges of producing this particular product (which most of Them had to conceive of as similar to and a more complex version of the designing and producing and promoting and selling of the garments, in that other Industry out of which so many of Them came and which, therefore, served as the foundation of and the model for that first generation of American filmmakers), They loved the pure and simple crapshoot and roulette whirl of it, loved the game in and of itself, the points of it, winning and losing, loved the gamble most of all. Is it any wonder that so many prominent people in the movie industry, then and now, have been literal gamblers as well, throwing away ransoms and fortunes at the tables of Las Vegas, Reno, Tahoe, Monaco? They love the action. More, finally, than the results. This is something They share with artists. Of course, that was the very heart of the Depression, when Faulkner was working on *The Road to Glory* and learning how to tell a hawk from a handsaw in Hollywood, and, as the late Sam Goldwyn once remarked, "We have passed a lot of water under the bridge since then." But Faulkner's advice was offered twenty years later, as the next generation came to power in Hollywood, the second generation.

The second generation, and now the third already, is disguised behind college educations, good tailoring, all the outward and visible benefits of expensive upbringing, health, and welfare. They are slicker, smoother, maybe as clever and far less flamboyantly colorful than their real and metaphorical parents. These barbarians wear togas and look good in them. But the game is the same and the risks are the same. And, as Faulkner suggested, the best thing to do when dealing with Them, moving among Them, is to take Them very seriously. On the strength of my own admiration for the mind and sensibility of William Faulkner, and out of my experience of his work, I can only conclude that he meant, too, that, weighing all, beyond all risks and rewards, these people deserve to be taken seriously, that They can be of both interest and value to the artist who can go beyond the garment-truth of stereotypes and clichés and open himself to what is wonderfully different. Faulkner was always fascinated by passionate and obsessed characters, characters who want something, love something. He could see this obsession and desire in the people who make the movies.

He seems to have known and understood enough, more than enough, to have written a really first-rate Hollywood novel. And it would be fun if there were one, one we could put alongside Fitzgerald's and O'Hara's and Nathanael West's. He took the people seriously enough. But I think it is clear that he didn't love Them enough, or the work either, to want to do it. He came and went. He endured and finally prevailed. Instead of a work about Hollywood, we have examples of his work for Hollywood. Which, in a real sense, offers its own commentary.

His advice to a young writer has its parallel in the tenth chapter of Matthew. *Behold, I send you as sheep in the midst of wolves: be ye therefore wise as serpents and innocent as doves.*

Faulkner was faced with another problem, a special kind of problem, in writing the script. There are still (probably always will be) unanswered questions about the nature and details of this adaptation. But it seems that the property which Zanuck had acquired, and now wished to develop into a script and an original film, was not a story idea, not a book or a play to be adapted, but rather an existing French movie, *Les Croix de Bois* (1932), itself said to be based upon the story line of a French novel. It appears that Zanuck was chiefly interested in using some of the extensive and expensive combat scenes from the French film, incorporating them as stock footage in his own film. So it became the assignment of the American screenwriters to come up with a story line and structure (in which task it is said that Howard Hawks contributed some anecdotes and reminiscences) which would make the most efficient and effective use of the footage from the French film. Early on in the script we see scene headings—"(STOCK C. de B.)"— which indicate that stock footage is to be used. Fairly soon, however, that heading is simply dropped, and it remains uncertain as to how much, if any, of the French combat footage was actually used in the American film.

Here a brief digression on the state of this particular script is called for. The opening sequence, and several other places, have the detail of camera angle and transition written in and thus have the look of a *final shooting script*, broken down into its smallest, component parts. Soon, however, we get *master scenes*, units of a page and more sometimes, with or without any indicated transition. Brief specific shots—see, for instance, scenes 37, 38, and 39—are indicated only to make story points or character reactions. Later (see, for example, scene 204) there are fairly long master scenes not broken down into individual shots. And in some places (see 215, 216, and following) there are scenes which are not scenes at all, really, but rather are synoptic sequences. There is nothing unusual about this. Several stages of development are represented in this script. In some places it could, conceivably, be shot as is. In other places there is a good deal of work, by several hands, left to be done before it is ready.

The idea of a script at this stage of development requires, among other things, that it should look like a final script, that it can and should be read more or less like a final shooting script. All these camera angles and directions, as well as the means of transition from one scene or shot to the next, even though these details may well have been suggested by the producers and the director, are really expendable. The cinematographer and the editor will, later, have a lot to say about those things. Meantime, though, the details give a sense of the *style* that the picture will probably have. And they give a not wholly inaccurate impression that the film script is almost finished. It can be read and budgeted, roughly, by those whose business it is to estimate schedules and costs. Can be read by investors, agents, actors, technicians, and so forth.

The writers have here established a basic story line, a general structure (this, of course, can change in shooting and in editing); and they have created the central characters. At this stage, dialogue (what they call "the words," as in "The leading man could not learn the words") is apt to be, as it is, fairly full, making plot and character points, where necessary, as overtly and as clearly as possible. Later, in the acting, shooting, and editing much of this may well be changed. Words can be added where points are not made or are not clear. Words can be cut where, thanks to acting, direction, and context, they are redundant. At this point the script remains primarily the work of the writers and is as close to being a *literary* document as a movie, in its metamorphosis of many shapes, can be. It is at this stage that the contributions of the screenwriting are most evident and important.

There are some wonderful cinematic moments and devices here which, whether or not they were able to survive to appear in the film itself, set a style and tone for it. The arrival of Pierre Delaage (scenes 8–20) by means of a hearse to join the Fifth Company of the Second Battalion of the Thirty-ninth Regiment is an excellent example. It immediately catches attention and establishes Pierre as a lively and sympathetic character. It is, moreover, exactly appropriate to both the form and the content of what follows, establishing that this war is almost more myth than fact, even for those most actively engaged in it. It makes the point, among others, visually and dramatically, that the differences between the living and the dead, thus between living and dying, are at once less clearly defined and more a matter of accident than anyone might wish to allow. This is good movie writing.

And there are other things, the Old Man's bugle, for instance, and the Captain's set speech to all new recruits, among many other similar devices throughout, which depend upon repetition to work their rhetorical, cinematic effects. (Those familiar with other Faulkner scripts—*The Big Sleep*, *To Have and Have Not*, and *Air Force*, for instance—will recall how he liked to use echoed and repeated phrases and actions to establish an intimacy with the characters and the experience.) These also serve to emphasize the cyclical nature of the action, a particularly important point in *The Road to Glory*, where the war is seen as an unending cycle. And there are any number of well-executed cinematic and dramatic sequences here. The sequence dealing with the mining beneath the dugout, beginning with scene 59, through the sudden silence and then the noise of digging again in 64 and 65, is powerful and effective. The bombing of the village (scenes 87–100) leading into the sequence of Pierre and Monique together in the cellar (101–20, with intercuts) is almost textbook screenwriting. And there are a whole series of strong dramatic scenes, fully realized. In short, the script seems to me to be at the very least a solid, workmanlike job, well constructed and full of interesting details. Faulkner was worth what they paid him.

Yet, having said that, it remains to be said that the real job of the writer is not, in fact, a matter of cinematic devices and gimmicks (whether they are good or not) or even, finally, of dramatic writing. What the writer must do is create characters and situations in which those characters can be tested and developed. And out of all this, deriving from his story line, emerges an attitude towards the material. There may or may not be a "message" in a movie. That depends. But there will almost always be a *statement* of one kind or another, even if that statement is primarily manifest as an attitude. Here is where, I believe, William Faulkner really gave them their money's worth and where we, who are mainly interested in how this screenplay fits into his life's work and relates to it, should focus our most serious attention.

the *New York Times* review (6 August 1936), by Frank S. Nugent, of the released picture gives us a good place to start. It is a mixed review, really, praising the skill of the picture makers while criticizing the implications of the story, the apparent statement it seemed to be making. Nugent allows that the treatment of war in this movie, "objective, but romanticized," is unacceptable after the experience of Erich Maria Remarque's *All Quiet on the Western Front*, Humphrey Cobb's *Paths of Glory* (which would much later be made into an exceptional film from a screenplay by Calder Willingham), and Irwin Shaw's play *Bury the Dead*. Nugent criticized Faulkner and Sayre for writing their screenplay "with the impersonality of a veteran newspaper man's account of a fire" and was disturbed by what he inferred, from "the swift chronicling of these disassociated events," to be the principal theme of the story, namely "the glory of service, of regimental tradition, selfless discipline and sacrifice." He went on to say that the audience had "a right to expect something more, a word or two, perhaps, on the significance and ultimate value of their sacrifice." Exactly, then, what Faulkner did not, would not do. Nugent found it technically exciting and gripping, but, as it were, ideologically upsetting. This entirely honest, if naïve, reaction gives us a good deal to consider.

First, it seems to me typical of Faulkner that he should create something against the grain of the current literary fashions in treating the subject. This demands that the writer be fully familiar with the literary conventions and clichés he would either use or discard. In everything he did, poetry, prose, fiction, essays, even the screenplays, Faulkner shows on the one hand a considerable, indeed an unusual familiarity with the precise literary fashions of the times and, on the other hand, a clear determination to distinguish his own work from those fashions by seeking to approach subjects (and forms) freshly, in new and different ways. Poetry, as it has been practiced in America in this century, did not give him the freedom or the room to do much. I am convinced that, even in the limited terms of verse writing, Faulkner was a better poet than has been allowed, but that the poets did not then and do not now understand what he was trying to do with their forms. The novel gave him the most opportunity, so that he was able to explore that form for all his working lifetime without ever repeating himself. Film, as a form of narrative, did not offer him as much latitude as prose fiction; but at least he could apply some of the same energies, albeit in the cruder, simpler forms of the screenplay.

In everything Faulkner created (as I see it), Faulkner showed great familiarity with the habits and fashions of a given form, or a given subject and its usual treatment, together with a strong impulse to distinguish his work by shattering as many of the habits and habitual reactions as he could. The reason behind this artistic impulse seems to have been the simple realization that habitual thinking and feeling, no matter how moral or uplifting, are the enemies of truth. He wanted, like Mark Twain, only differently, always *differently*, to tell the truth, mainly. *The Road to Glory* tells the truth, as best it could be told in this form, about the experience of war.

It is a strange thing that in this century of wars, wars in which millions and millions have been involved, our intellectuals and critics (and, alas, so many of our artists) seem to have learned so little, to know so little about war. Faulkner knew something about it all without being there except in his unflagging imagination. He wore a uniform, he served a time; and if he never did go overseas and into combat, he didn't have to. He learned enough and knew enough to understand war as well as any others who have written about it. And he wrote very well about war—in the stories of World War I, like "Turnabout" and "Ad Astra." In the novels—*Sol-*

diers' Pay, Sartoris, The Unvanquished, A Fable, and so forth—he showed, it seems to me, a deeper comprehension of the texture of the experience of war, and its after-effects, than did Hemingway in *A Farewell to Arms* or *For Whom the Bell Tolls.* (*Across the River and Into the Trees* comes closer to Faulkner.)

As late as the recent war in Vietnam, people who ought to know better were discussing the rights and wrongs of warfare, acting as if one side or the other in a war was strengthened or weakened by moral or ethical considerations. Acting as if ideology has ever had anything to do with survival. Believing that there are "good" wars and "bad" ones. Every soldier who has experienced combat knows that ideology, the Cause (whatever it may be), morality, and ethics are not so much expendable as utterly inessential. At best as ludicrously out of date as the Old Man's battered bugle. Scenes 170 and 171, in which Morache and Regnier examine the packs and equipment of the new replacements and order them to get rid of everything that is not essential, make this point. "We see that their equipment is in sharp contrast to that of the veterans." This is a story about veterans. Not about the "meaning" of sacrifice. Not even a statement against war. Which would be completely irrelevant. War speaks out against itself. And, in truth, war is the only life these people know and experience, while we know and experience them, until they die. War is shown to be unending. The cycle goes on and on, attack and retreat, without any hope of a conclusion. There may be intervals of peace and quiet, of love and festivity, but the war is always there.

In that sense, *The Road to Glory* is as much prophetic truth as it is accurate history. Mid-thirties—Hitler already in power and arming, Mussolini seeking empire in Africa, Japan at war in China, Stalin preparing for war and meantime purging and slaughtering his own people, merciless. *The Road To Glory* becomes, in retrospect, an allegory for our times. Without ideology, Cause, honest historical memory, or any real hope for the future, for any future, what was left for these people? Duty and honor among comrades remained. That is all that is left for the veteran soldier, his loyalty not to a nation or an idea, but to his fellows. Duty, honor, courage, and, on occasion, compassion remain. And love, if and when it can be found, though both Delaage and Morache are willing to give up love out of a deeper sense of honor. There are no true heroes, though Morache is shown to be exemplary throughout, the finished veteran. There is only one real villain. The man who trades in evil, for whom war is commerce, is the orderly Bouffiou. He is shown to be a coward and a conniver who can profit from the misery of others. The scene (177) where he burns the Old Man's orders, for a price, mixes disobedience with commerce and is, in fact, presented as the most wicked single act in this story. Much as Jason's burning of the circus tickets in *The Sound and The Fury* is the most wicked act in that tragic story.

What I am suggesting is that, within the limits of the conventions of the war story, this screenplay is remarkable for its integrity and its authenticity. It is a pared down, tough story. It is about as ruthlessly unsentimental as it could possibly be and still qualify for release and distribution as a major motion picture. Soon enough, after revisions and polish, with the aid of Howard Hawks's direction and with the benefit of a superb cast (Warner Baxter as the Captain, Lionel Barrymore as the Old Man, his father, and Fredric March as the Lieutenant) it was made into an outstanding motion picture, one of our finest, then or now, on the subject of men at war, and one which has clearly influenced many later films. The whole process began with the story and this script. There are faults and flaws in the script. There always are. And there was still time to correct many of these in revision. But the story line, the tone and truth of it, was absolutely essential to the success of the movie. Faulkner earned his money, finished *Absalom, Absalom!* and headed home. With still many years to go before he would receive any recognition for the work he had done, was doing, and would continue to do.

He was, in a way, like a figure in his own story. It was, like most good stories, just that personal in implication, though well disguised. Something of him was the Old Man with his bugle and his dreams of old glories. Something of him was as weary, as battered, and as dutiful as the Captain. Something was still young, at that time, as lively and sardonic, as fond of whiskey and love and the quixotic gesture as the Lieutenant. And something in him deeply understood Bouffiou; for here he was, making commerce of his art, selling his time in an effort to earn more free time for himself, trying to survive at all costs.

If nothing else, this screenplay proves he had the ability to survive and to persevere, by hard labor, on his own. It proves, among other things, that he could do a job on order and for hire, when he had to. It proves here to be a good job, one worthy of the gifts of the man who was also writing *Absalom, Absalom!* at the same time. If nothing else, the quality of this work should change the picture of Faulkner as someone who was "carried" by and through the kindness of Howard Hawks. That may have been the case later (who knows?). But here he did the job right and made Hawks look good. A good script makes everyone involved look good. It is always a gamble, but when Hawks hired Faulkner later on, he was betting on a winner. And I would guess he knew it.

Textual Note

Copy-text for this edition of *The Road to Glory* is the mimeographed typescript by Joel Sayre and William Faulkner dated 31 December 1935. The movie was produced from a later screenplay revised by Sayre and Nunnally Johnson, with new scenes by Faulkner and Howard Hawks.

Spelling, punctuation, and obvious typing errors have been corrected; and the camera directions have been regularized. In directions and speech headings the characters' names have been substituted for descriptive identifications ("Nervous Soldier" becomes Ledoux). Variant spellings of names have been made consistent (Bouffioux/Bouffiou, Delage/Delaage, Marache/Morache).

The following substantive emendations have been made in the dialogue.

16.21, 22; 34; 17.15; 21.9, 13   Three [Four
20.16   Third [Fourth
40.11   of [or
50.0   Bosh [Boche

50.4   machine barrage [machine-gun barrage

53.10   than [that

80.9   Neigh [Ney

81.13-14, 30; 84.15; 85.12   139th [Thirty-ninth

81.34   combat since [combat unit since

82.1   add a statute [add stature

82.2-3   detract that [detract from that

89.5   attach [attack

89.21   Fifth [Second

90.20   it [is

91.6   La Coste [Achard

111.27   of mine [of the mine

120.13   cowardice [coward

132.19   to [the

132.26   five after two now [five now

157.5   139th [39th

The speech at 33.23 has been transferred from Rigaud to Regnier.

Joel Sayre was a colorful reporter, World War II War correspondent, satirical novelist, and screenwriter. Among his screen work in addition to *The Road to Glory* were *Gunga Din* and *Annie Oakley*.

William Faulkner, Nobel laureate and giant of twentieth-century American literature, at different periods in his life worked out of financial necessity as a screenwriter. While collaborating on *The Road to Glory* he completed a draft of *Absalom, Absalom!*

George Garrett is a poet, playwright, novelist, screenwriter, and former professor who now devotes himself full-time to his writing at his home in York Harbor, Maine.